The Visitor's Guide
to the
COTSWOLDS

INDEX TO 1:50 000 MAPS OF GREAT BRITAIN

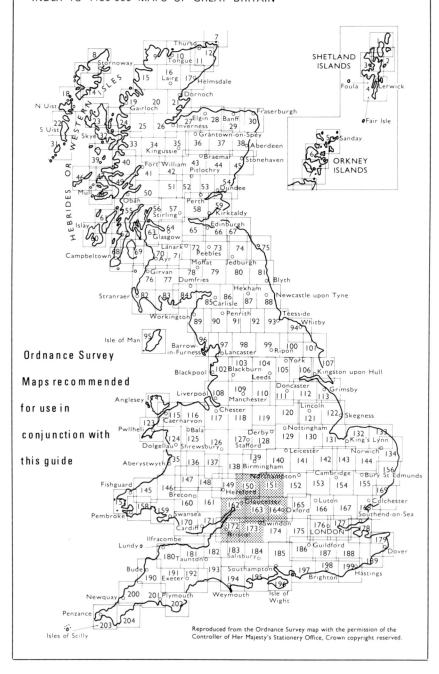

Ordnance Survey

Maps recommended

for use in

conjunction with

this guide

The Visitor's Guide To
THE
COTSWOLDS

Richard Sale

MPC

HUNTER
PUBLISHING INC

British Library Cataloguing in
Publication Data

Sale, Richard, 1946–
The visitor's guide to the
Cotswolds. — 2nd ed.
1. Cotswold Hills
(England) — Description
and travel — Guide-books.
I. Title
914.24′1704858   DA670.C83

Photographs on pages 12, 14, 15, 22, 35, 37,
42, 44, 47, 48, 52, 53 (lower), 65, 68, 90, 98,
115, 118, 120, 121 are by J. A. Robey; p80 by
Robert Opie Collection; the remainder were
taken by the author.
Colour illustrations have been supplied
by: L. Porter (Moreton-in-Marsh, Stow-
on-the Wold); J. A. Robey (Bath,
Chipping Campden, Hidcote Manor); the
remainder are by the author.

First edition 1982
Reprinted 1983
Revised edition 1987

Published in the UK by
Moorland Publishing Co Ltd,
Ashbourne, Derbyshire,
Tel: (0335) 44486

ISBN 0 86190 158 4 (paperback)
ISBN 0 86190 159 2 (hardback)

Published in the USA by
Hunter Publishing Inc,
300 Raritan Center Parkway,
CN94, Edison, NJ 08818

ISBN 0 935161 50 3 (paperback)

Printed in the UK by
Butler and Tanner Ltd,
Frome, Somerset.

Contents

Notes on the Walks Described
The walks suggested are not intended to be field-by-field guides, but general indications of worthwhile outings. It is assumed that the walker possesses the relevant 1.50,000 series OS map.

In addition the interested visitor would find it worthwhile to obtain the Gloucestershire Ramblers' Association's maps on public rights-of-way in the county; they cover the greater part of the Cotswold Area. It must be recognised that there is little common land in the area, and that the walks follow rights-of-way across private farm land. The Cotswolds are not a mountainous area, but may still spring the odd surprise on the walker; so it is wise to be prepared.

For each walk the distance and estimated time is given, together with the information below:

T	Town Walk
W	Wold route. Since these will include a measure of upland walking they could be weather-swept
V	Valley route. Usually less weather-swept
o	Of least interest
oo	
ooo	
oooo	Of most interest
*	Well signposted and easily followed
**	Requires a knowledge of rights-of-way to follow

Places of tourist interest which may be visited are indicated alongside the text with the symbols shown in the adjacent key. Opening times and other details may be found in the Further Information on pages 124–38.

Key for Maps

 Towns/Villages

 Motorways

 Mainroads

 Rivers

 Lakes/Reservoirs

 Zoo/Animal Interest

 Museum/Art Gallery

 Church

 Archaeological Site

 Building

 Country Park

 Garden

 Nature Reserve/Trail

 Other Place of Interest

6

The Cotswolds

The Ordnance Survey insists, on the maps of the area east of the River Severn, that the uplands are known as the Cotswold Hills. This is not strictly true, as there are no hills. The true name is The Cotswolds, which not only drops the offending word, but also accurately describes the area, the word *wold* being old English for 'an upland common'.

The Cotswolds are, geologically, a limestone mass, but it is not the Carboniferous Limestone which dissolves so easily in water and which forms the gorges and caves of the nearby Mendips. Cotswold limestone is Oolitic, which means 'egg-stone' in Greek, and is representative of the stone: a fish roe-like mass of small granules. Since such limestones are laid down beneath sea, there are also a large number of fossils in the rock. This, together with the relative softness of the rock, allows the fossils to be easily extracted, and makes the exposures of the rock happy hunting grounds for the fossil-hunter. The most accessible areas are Cleeve Hill, on the side of the A46, and Leckhampton Hill.

The limestone mass has been split by river valleys, the water cutting the valleys rather than dissolving them, and this gives the appearance of hills; as does the collection of 'outliers' to the west of the main rock mass. The geography of the area is typically limestone — the scarp slope, or escarpment, produced by erosion on one side (here, the west) and a long shallow slope, the dip, on the other. The formation of a scarp slope by erosion frequently leaves behind outliers which are lumps of harder, less easily weathered, rock. The most striking is Bredon Hill, but other smaller masses are Churchdown and Robins Wood Hill near Gloucester. Further south, the effect can be seen quite strikingly near

Dursley, where, to the north, Cam Peak and Cam Long Down are 'recently' created outliers, while to the south Stinchcombe Hill has been narrowed to only a few yards at a point some 800yd back from the main scarp slope.

The rock, at least the so-called 'freestone', has long been a source of considerable wealth for the area. When newly quarried, it is soft and can be cut readily with a saw, but on exposure to the air it hardens. It therefore has great advantages as a building stone, and was extensively used in the Middle Ages, for example in St Paul's Cathedral. As the stone split easily it produced roof tiles. The splitting was mainly produced by natural causes, the stone being stored wet by laying wet sacks over it. When the winter frosts came, it was exposed and the water froze in the cracks. Thawing later caused the rock to shatter, and as the cracks were usually even and parallel, slates were formed. They were very thick, however, and a roof required the support of huge oak beams; trade rapidly diminished when Welsh slates became readily available. Today the production of Cotswold building stone is on a much reduced scale. But its variety of colour, from golden-brown to pale grey, still makes it attractive where price is not the dominant factor.

The derivation of 'Cot' is more difficult. Some authorities believe it may derive from the word for a 'sheep enclosure', and that is certainly appropriate in view of the medieval usage of the wolds. Others dispute this, pointing out that in earlier times the name was used only for a very tiny portion of what is now the Cotswolds. They contend that the name derives from *Cod*, pronounced 'code', a Saxon leader who farmed around the headwaters of the Windrush some 1,200

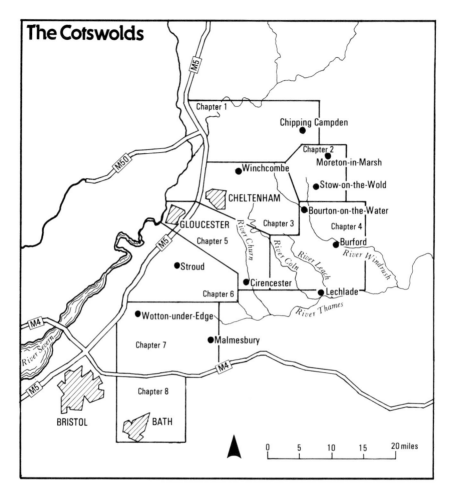

The Cotswolds

or more years ago. The name Cotswold would then be 'Cod's high land', and nearby Cutsdean would derive its name from the same root. If the latter derivation is correct, it explains why the name was at first applied only to the area around the source of the Windrush, reaching the Stroud valley by the late nineteenth century, and extending to cover the geologically and geographically similar areas south to Bath only in very recent times. It would also appeal to the romantic, for the Windrush is the most essentially Cotswold of all the rivers that split the wolds. By the time of Cod, if we accept the fact of his existence, the area was already steeped in history. The earliest inhabitants were early Stone Age hunters following the animals in the forests that grew here after the last Ice Age. These early forests of pine and birch gave way later to oak, elm and beech. The beeches, now such a spectacular feature of the central area of the region, were crucially important to the Neolithic, or New Stone Age, man, the first to settle in the area, for it was on the beech mast that the Neolithic farmer's pigs fed. The farmers also cleared the forest and cultivated the fertile wold soil, and it was they who left the first permanent memorial to man's involvement in the area — the long barrows. Such is the importance of the area's barrows — over 100 of them — that they form a specific class — the Severn-Cotswold group. It is difficult to be definite about such structures, but the interested visitor should try to see Belas Knap, Hetty Pegler's Tump (or Uley Tumulus as it is officially called) and Notgrove. Perhaps the most interesting feature of the barrows, which are actually burial chambers, is that although they are basically chambers of stone slabs, covered with earth, they usually have a doorway flanked by horns of dry-stone walling. There is a noticeable continuity, over 4,000-5,000 years, between this work and modern stone-walling. In the Bronze Age the area was of only limited importance: interments were now in round barrows — the best example, unquestionably, being Nan Tow's Tump near Oldbury-on-the-Hill.

The defensive advantages of the area, with its many promontories, were realised by the Iron Age people. They built a great number of hillforts along the Cotswold edge. One of the best, in terms of remains, is at Little Sodbury, although the extensive excavations at Crickley Hill have made it the best understood. The biggest is at Minchinhampton, on the edge of the Stroud valley and just outside the official Cotswold area. Here the remnants of the Iron Age tribesmen, fleeing north from the invading Romans, made a last stand, and were annihilated. It is easy to regard the coming of Rome as the march of civilisation over a few pagan savages, but the Birdlip mirror, now in Gloucester Museum, shows that the Iron Age tribes of the Cotswolds included skilled craftsmen, and were undoubtedly highly civilised.

The fine remains at Cirencester and Bath, and at the villas at Chedworth and Woodchester, show how much the Romans liked the area. Bath was, of course, tailor-made for a people whose social life revolved around bathing, but the main reason for the area's importance was, again, strategic. The high wold-land was easily defended, particularly on its western (the most vulnerable) flank, and many important highways were built across it — the Foss Way, Ermin Street, Akeman Street and others. Its importance was later recognised by the Saxons, reaching the Cotswolds around AD600, after a decisive battle at Dyrham. Gloucester and Winchcombe now became very important, standing on the Mercia-Wessex border, and the Cotswolds were the high level route between these two strong, and occasionally hostile, kingdoms. Such was the area's importance, in fact, that Gloucester could well have become the capital of England, had not the Normans arrived and transferred central power to London and the south-east.

The number and wealth of the abbeys and churches show the continued importance of the area: but 200 years later that importance increased, again for a geographical reason. On the wolds a local breed of sheep — the Cotswold — fared very well, producing a 28lb-fleece. The rivers, in their steep valleys, provided power for mills, and large deposits of fuller's earth fulfilled the basic need of cloth-making.

At first the important item was the fleece itself, which was exported raw to continental Europe. There its full importance was realised, the Duke of Burgundy instituting the Order of the Golden Fleece. Soon however Edward III 'began to grow sensible of the great gain the Netherlands got by our English wool'. 'Golden Fleece' was indeed a true description — the fleece was English, the gold was Europe's. So Flemish weavers were brought to England to start a woollen industry. In a few years it dominated the English economy, being by far the largest single item. The Cotswolds produced more than half the cloth; every other worker in the area was involved in the industry in some way.

The area had over 500,000 sheep and the shepherds were very important. They received a bowl of whey daily in summer, the milk of ewes on Sundays, a lamb at weaning, and a fleece at shearing.

The shepherds were important, but it was the merchants who were rich, some almost beyond our comprehension, even lending money to the king, as they had more of it than the Exchequer. They built fine houses, but their chief method of spending was the endowment of churches — the wool churches. All over the Cotswolds fine buildings were erected and stocked with treasures, and then with the tombs of the merchants themselves. No visit to the area is complete without a pilgrimage to the churches of Cirencester, Northleach and Chipping Campden. But many others are minor treasure houses, and the inquisitive visitor will be well rewarded. The merchants knew where the prime source of their income was — one merchant's house being inscribed:

I praise God and ever shall
It is the sheep hath paid for it all

The Government was well aware of this wealth; the Lord Chancellor still sits on a woolsack.

This trade lasted several centuries, but when it ended the devastation was appalling. Whole families starved to death; others survived long enough to move out of the area; the poverty was awful. Ironically it was this poverty that made the Cotswolds a tourist area. The lack of development in the towns and villages after the seventeenth and eighteenth centuries meant that they were not modernised in any way, and rows of beautiful, old buildings can still be seen in, for example Chipping Campden High Street.

Lately the region has been designated an Area of Outstanding Natural Beauty, shortened to AONB for the remainder of this book. The AONB follows the Cotswold edge from near Bath to Chipping Campden, and includes Bredon Hill. To the east it follows roughly the line of the Foss Way. Many feel that in the east the AONB should extend further into Oxfordshire, but in a book such as this it is necessary to draw a line somewhere. Only the official area has been considered, except where certain places of significant interest lie within a very short distance of the boundary.

The visitor to the Cotswolds need never be short of something to do. In good weather he may follow rivers, explore villages and visit viewpoints, and if it rains, the interest of all members of the family may be kept by visits to buildings and museums. Neither is it all food for the mind, as a tourist information sheet 'Eating out in the Cotswolds' mentions some excellent restaurants.

The Cotswolds are about people and buildings, and differ in that respect from other tourist areas, notably the mountainous National Parks. Many of the walks described in this book are centred around villages. A newcomer to the area, more used to the empty silence of the hills, will find that these suggested walks, like the Cotswolds themselves, are most rewarding.

1 The North-Western Edge

The position of the Cotswolds, situated centrally between the Midlands and the South-West of England, between Wales and the Oxford Plain, means that there is no true 'gateway' to the area. The geography of the area (for there are no hills in the Cotswold Hills — the name is misleading) also allows the visitor to be well within the boundaries of the designated Area of Outstanding Natural Beauty (AONB) before he is aware that he has arrived. Only if coming from the west, and, to a lesser extent from the north, is a noticeable change discerned as one first approaches, and then ascends the limestone escarpment that is the Cotswolds. So let us begin by starting from a point where one can, with a walk of little over three miles, grasp the essential elements that make up the Cotswolds, their scenery and

history.

The starting point is the car park of the National Trust site on Dover's Hill, a little way north-west of Chipping Campden. After going left out of the car park and down to the crossroads one turns right along the road signposted for Broadway and Willersey and a little way along the road crosses to the left side, to look down and back. There, nestling in a gently wooded valley, is the town of **Chipping Campden**. It is a typically Cotswold town and from this vantage point the essential 'typical Cotswold' features are apparent. First is the stone, pale grey and cream limestone. The distinctive geography of the area, and the distinctive appearance of the houses are due to this same limestone. The second feature is the church. Almost all Cotswold towns and villages are

W
3m
1h
oooo
*

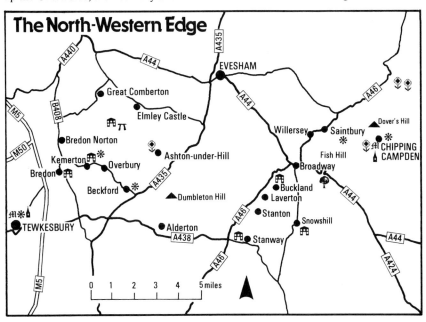

The North-Western Edge

Chipping Campden Church

dominated by marvellous churches bequeathed by the rich wool merchants. Again geography has played a part; the high wolds, or common land areas, together with the streams that run from them, produced the wealth of the Cotswolds in the late Middle Ages. The sheep that fed on the wolds produced the wool that formed the basis of the economy of England, and the merchants who traded in it were incredibly rich. They vied with each other, not to build lavish buildings for themselves, (although fine houses were built) but to raise and decorate churches, the 'wool' churches. The church at Chipping Campden is perhaps the finest 'wool' church in the Cotswolds.

Chipping Campden

Continuing along the road, the visitor reaches, tucked away in woodland to the right, the Kiftsgate Stone, which is, in its way, as remarkable as the wool churches themselves. This is a 'moot' point, a place where the people of the area could gather to discuss business, hold court, or hear of important events. The 'gate' in the name is not to be taken literally; there is no gate, the word deriving from the Saxon for 'track'. But if Saxon times seem long ago, one must remember that when the name was given to this stone it was probably as ancient to the Saxons as they are to us. Few areas in Britain can claim to have a longer and consistently more important history than the Cotswolds. From this spot the proclamation of George III was read, probably the last great event recorded here. At the same time as the woollen industry was declining, so were the Cotswolds. Unhappy as this decline was for those who worked in the industry, its result has been that the villages and towns are now as they were then, and so have maintained their charm, a charm

that would undoubtedly have been lost if continuous prosperity had resulted in the continuous modernisation of old houses, and the building of new.

Returning to the car park, the visitor can now go across to the panorama dial from where he will enjoy not only an expansive vista over the Vale of Evesham to the Malvern Hills, but also a nearby view along the northern edge of the escarpment. Here the true geography of the Cotswolds is seen; there are no hills at all; it is only this escarpment which rises to over one thousand feet in its more northerly reaches; being cut by river valleys, it has the appearance of hills. If the escarpment here is sudden, the dip slope behind is not, falling the same thousand feet over a distance of many miles, towards the Upper Thames Valley. Those, therefore, who approach from the east can be deep into the Cotswolds before they realise that they have gained any height at all.

The first of the town walks in this book starts at Chipping Campden. Here a short walk takes in the better parts of

T
1½m
oooo
*

13

Thatched cottages at Westington, near Chipping Campden

the town itself, and also visits the picturesque and very *non*-Cotswold thatched cottages of Westington, reached from Sheep Street. The itinerary for any visitor to Chipping Campden must include St James' church, not only because it is such a fine example of a 'wool' church, and so structurally perfect, but because of the wealth of its treasures and curios inside. Most noticeable perhaps is the Grevel brass, commemorating William Grevel (who died in 1401) and his wife. The brass is the largest, and one of the oldest, in Gloucestershire. Especially notable is the craftsmanship with which Grevel's wife is depicted: her dress is closed with over eighty buttons, each individually formed. Equally interesting are the life-size alabaster effigies of Sir Baptist and Lady Elizabeth Hicks in the South Chapel. They lie in their coronation robes and are overlooked by two more life-size figures of their eldest daughter and her husband in funeral shrouds,

hand-in-hand, arising from their tomb on judgement day. Other busts of the Hicks family adorn the walls, the whole chapel being virtually a private mausoleum. Sir Baptist Hicks was one of the great wool merchants of his day, with immense wealth. Indeed he was so rich that he often lent vast sums to King James I. His London house commemorated this Gloucestershire village, giving its name to the area — Campden Hill Square — and his bequests raised some of the more interesting buildings in the town, including the almshouses near the church and the Market Hall in the centre of High Street. William Grevel's house remains in High Street. It is over six hundred years old, and opposite it is one that is equally old — Woolstaplers' Hall. This was the meeting place of the staple, (i.e. fleece), merchants and it now houses an interesting museum of the woollen industry and other country crafts. There are also exhibits on the history of

Village pump at Chipping Campden

PLACES OF INTEREST AROUND
BROADWAY AND CHIPPING CAMPDEN

Buckland Rectory, Buckland
England's oldest working rectory.
The house contains a fifteenth
century great hall

Hidcote Manor Gardens, Hidcote
Bartrim
Gardens by Major Lawrence
Johnston. Many small gardens, each
individually walled. Also rare trees,
shrubs and a rose collection.

Kiftsgate Court Gardens
Gardens only open to the public.
Very fine shrub and rose collections

Snowshill Manor
Restored Tudor house. 'Magpie'
collections of musical instruments,
clocks, toys, bicycles and much more.

**Woolstaplers Hall Museum, Chipping
Campden**
Display of the history of the town,
and collection of dentists'
instruments and survey equipment

Broadway Tower Country Park
Excellent park with nature trails;
exhibits on natural history and
country crafts. Tower offers fine view

Fish Hill Picnic Site
Panorama Dial

Kiftsgate Stone
Ancient moot point

Ernest Wilson Memorial Gardens
Chinese and Japanese Shrubs

photography and of dentistry.
The visitor who has started at St
James' Church and has then entered
High Street near Grevel House and
Woolstaplers' Hall, can now walk down
what has been called the show-piece of
the Cotswolds. Almost every house has a
notable history and the wide street has
occasional buildings in its centre
including the early sixteenth century
Hicks Market Hall and the partly
fourteenth century Town Hall.
The arrival in 1902 of the Guild of
Handicrafts in the town has stimulated
the establishment of many craft
workshops; local shops have examples
of the work. One workshop that can be
visited is the pottery in the Leysbourne
district, at the Church end of High
Street. The shop on the premises also
sells the work of other local craft
workers, together with work from
further afield. In Calf Lane, which runs
parallel to High Street, there are
footpaths that lead to two old mills still
complete with their large, overshot
water-wheels.

Chipping Campden is also a good
centre for short expeditions to other,
smaller, villages on the northern edge of
the Cotswolds. To the north and east
there are a number of interesting places
that lie outside the AONB — there can

be few villages with a more Cotswold 'feel' than Ebrington, or Ilmington (which is held to be home of Cotswold Morris Dancing). Ebrington can be reached by path from Campden; the return journey by the lane running south from the village is a good introduction to country lane walking in the Cotswolds. Ebrington, apart from being a delightful village, is also the butt of local 'village idiot' jokes. Here they manured the church tower to make it grow taller; it is the place where they boiled a donkey to get his harness off; it was a local who carried his wheelbarrow for seven miles so that the wheel would not dent the road; as if to agree, the locals refer to the village not by its correct name, but as Yubberton.

 Also within a short distance of Chipping Campden are the **Hidcote Manor Gardens**, near Mickleton, laid out over his lifetime by Major Lawrence Johnston and presented by him to the National Trust. Hidcote is especially interesting to the amateur gardener because it is not one large expanse, but a series of small gardens, each hedged around, and planted with a single class of flower. For those who love gardens the day can perhaps be rounded off with a visit to the more formal **Kiftsgate Court Gardens**, also close to Mickleton. There are rare shrubs here, and the collection of roses is one of the finest in Britain.

There is an enjoyable walk along the escarpment near **Dover's Hill**, on which the panorama dial identifies the points of interest in the Vale of Evesham below. The hill's name is from Robert Dover, a local lawyer who in the early 1600s created the Cotswold 'olympick' games there. The games were famous in their day; they had the royal seal of approval and were mentioned by Shakespeare, who possibly visited them. The actual events would probably not be recognised by the current Olympic committee, who would scarely class as a sport either shin-kicking, or singlestick fighting, the object of which was to break your opponent's head with your staff before he did the same to you. Neither would they like the boisterous good-humour, of competitors and spectators alike, which led to the eventual prohibition of the games in the mid-nineteenth century. By then the boisterousness had become riots, with vandalism in Chipping Campden. The open land that now affords such fine views of the edge and vale is only a small part of the original games area and was bought by the National Trust in 1928. On the National Trust plaque in the car park is a portrait of a man on a white horse, in a suit with a feathered hat, probably a picture of Robert Dover himself since it is known that King James gave him a similar suit and that he opened the games on a white horse, while cannons were fired from a mock fort. In 1951 the games, though not all the original sports, were revived. They are held on the eve of Scuttlebrook Wake, a Chipping Campden festival which includes the crowning of the May Queen held in the Market Square, on the Saturday following the Spring Holiday.

The Fish Inn, a curious building but a good pub, is a short walk from Chipping Campden. It is sited at the top of **Fish Hill** which takes the A44 into Broadway, opposite a picnic area. There is also a panorama dial and a nature trail. The picnic site has a warm, friendly, air in early summer, but this has not always been the case. In 1660 William Harrison, a steward employed by Lady Juliana Noel of Campden, the daughter of Sir Baptist Hicks whose tomb is in Campden Church, disappeared. A search of the area the following day revealed his blood-stained comb and hat-band, but no other trace of him. Because of the blood-stains, and because Harrison had been a rent-collector and was, therefore, carrying a large amount of money, foul play was suspected. Suspicion fell on John Perry, Harrison's manservant, whose behaviour on the night of the disappearance was curious. Perry had an alibi which was checked and found to be accurate, but then, astonishingly, during questioning his story changed and became increasingly bizarre. He first claimed Harrison had been murdered by a wandering tinker, and then that his mother, and brother Richard, had killed him. After further questioning, he admitted that he had been present when the murder was committed, but that his only action was to tell the others of Harrison's movements. To prove his story, he led his questioners to the millpond where the body had been thrown. The pond was dredged, but nothing was discovered. Despite this, and the protests of Mrs Perry and Richard, the three were accused of murder. The judge was obviously uneasy about the lack of a body and refused to try them, but early in 1661 a more enthusiastic judge was found, and the three were found guilty of murder and sentenced to death. They were executed near this spot in the early summer. A large crowd was present, and because of a local belief that Mrs Perry was a witch, she was hanged first, in case she had bewitched her sons and the spell might be broken. Before Richard died, his pleas to his brother were so impassioned that the crowd joined in shouting for John to admit his brother's innocence. John remained silent until his turn came, and then he too protested his innocence and that of his family. After his execution his body was left to rot in chains, also near this spot.

The body, or what remained of it, was still there two years later when William Harrison walked back into his home in Chipping Campden. He had a remarkable story to tell; of kidnappings and beatings; of being sold as a slave in Turkey, of escaping and fleeing across Europe to Portugal; of gaining passage on a boat to London; and of walking to Campden from there. The story is amazing enough, the more so when we consider that Harrison was about 70 at the time. Now, over 300 years later, it is hard to arrive at the truth, but the general opinion is that Harrison was embezzling money from the Noels, and

Broadway Tower

conspired with John Perry to fake a violent robbery when he feared that his crime would be discovered. Though this may be true, it leaves many questions unanswered. Why did Perry confess and why did he involve his family? And why did both Harrison and, even more remarkably, Perry remain silent through the trial, sentence and execution? There were those who doubted Harrison's story even then, but the Noels continued to employ him until he died aged over 80. After his return, his wife, who should have been overjoyed, even if shocked, committed suicide. The story can make the air seem cold at Fish Hill.

From the hill a walk that involves a good deal of uphill work follows the Cotswold Way to **Broadway Tower** and down into Broadway, returning by pathway over Willersey Hill, and its golf course, to the lane running southward across the high wold to the top of Fish Hill. Alternatively, a shortened walk, or a drive, can be made to Broadway

W
7½m
3h
oo
*

17

Prior's Manse, Broadway

Tower, which is now the centrepiece of the Tower Country Park, which is devoted exclusively to the study of the countryside.

There are two barns, each of original design, though reconstructed on site. One is an information centre; the other houses several exhibits on the local area, its geology, wildlife and country crafts, particularly the dry-stone walling for which the Cotswolds are famous. There are also two nature walks, one taking approximately half an hour, the other an hour. The tower itself has an interesting history: it was built in 1799 by the Earl of Coventry as a present for his wife, who was impressed that she was able to see a bonfire lit on Broadway Hill, part of their local estate, from their Worcestershire estate and wanted the tower as a permanent landmark and reminder of her Cotswold home. The view from the roof gallery is reputed, as are so many others, to be the most extensive in Britain. It is certainly true that before county boundaries were re-drawn thirteen counties could be seen

from the tower; the Wrekin and Welsh Hills are visible, as well as other nearer landmarks such as Worcester cathedral. Even with re-drawn boundaries twelve counties may be seen. The tower was not constructed of local stone, as the earl wanted it to be darker. Later repairs in the local, lighter, stone can easily be identified. Major repairs have been required several times, as the tower has fallen into disrepair. Once it was saved by the Pre-Raphaelite artists, Morris, Rossetti and Burne-Jones, and more recently by the Batsford Estate, who now run the Country Park.

Broadway itself, which is in Worcestershire rather than in Gloucestershire, is the tourist centre of the Cotswolds and has, as a result, a considerable number of shops. Most are aimed at the visitor, many being outlets for local craftsmen. The world-famous furniture factory of Gordon Russell is just off the main street. The village name derives, quite naturally, from the width of the main street. Its width is due to the covering of two streams that run down each side of the original, narrower road. When it was originally covered dip-holes were left for buckets as the village did not have piped water; they have been filled within living memory. Despite the high degree of commercialisation in the town, there is much that is very beautiful and fascinating. Especially notable is Prior's Manse, one of the oldest houses in Worcestershire. It was constructed in the fourteenth century for the Prior of Worcester, but the dormer windows give it a very modern look. The Lygon Arms commemorates General Lygon, a local eccentric who had his estate planted with clumps of trees in the same formation as the troops at the battle of Waterloo, so that he could re-enact the battle. The inn also commemorates Broadway's past as a staging post on the coaching route from Worcester to London. Because of the steepness of Fish Hill the stage coach stopped here to take on extra horses, and the town became a fashionable overnight stop. At the height of its

popularity the town, which was smaller than now, had more than twenty such inns.

To the north of Broadway are the villages of Willersey and Saintbury in Gloucestershire, not Worcestershire. **Saintbury** is built on the escarpment as it starts to swing eastwards, and there are fine views of the Vale of Evesham from above the town. **Willersey**, closer to the foot of the escarpment, has some typical North Cotswold stone cottages clustered around a duck pond and green.

Weston-sub-Edge was the home of William Latimer; his house, Latimer House, far older than any of the others in the village, still stands. Latimer was a friend of Sir Thomas More and Erasmus. He helped William Tyndale to translate the New Testament into English. He was a fine Greek scholar who promoted the study of Greek civilisation at Oxford, and translated the works of Aristotle. One of the cottages is called Ryknield, a reference to the

Lygon Arms, Broadway

Roman road — Ryknield Street — that passes close to the village.

At nearby **Aston-sub-Edge** is the Manor House, a fine building that was the home of Endymion Porter, a famous patron of the arts in the time before the Civil War, who was instrumental in the setting up of Robert Dover's games on the nearby escarpment. When Prince Rupert visited the games he stayed with Porter. His life of luxury came to an end with the Civil War, when he was banished as a Royalist and lived in great poverty in Holland. He eventually returned to England and is buried in the church of St Martin's-in-the-Field, London.

On the road to Cheltenham, between Broadway and Winchcombe, there is a collection of typical Cotswold villages strung out along the spring line at the base of the escarpment, with one, Snowshill, equally fine, set on the wold above them. The six villages — Buckland, Laverton, Snowshill, Stanton, Stanway and Didbrook are linked quite straightforwardly by path and bridleway, including a section of the Cotswold Way. From Laverton the walk goes across fields to Buckland, by a path up the escarpment to Buckland Wood, a track to Great Brockhampton Farm, and paths to Snowshill, Lidcombe Wood and on to the B4077. Going across fields to Wood Stanway and on to Didbrook, one can return to Stanway and follow the Cotswold Way to Stanton, finishing across fields to Laverton. Each of the villages is seen to perfection by the visitor as he moves up and down the scarp. **Laverton** is a quiet, almost secret, village, slightly bigger than **Buckland**, but having nothing to compare with the latter's rectory. This is probably the oldest and most complete 'working' parsonage in the country and possesses a stained-glass window from the mid-fifteenth century containing the arms of Edward IV.

Snowshill is renowned for its manor, now administered by the National Trust. It is interesting architecturally as a typical fifteenth/sixteenth-century manor house, with a very good

W
10
10m
3¾
ooc
**

Snowshill

dovecote. The gardens are terraced and have been designed as a series of cottage gardens, complete with rockeries and stone walls. Equally interesting is the 'Magpie Museum', which Mr Charles Wade left to the National Trust. There are vehicles of all sorts from bicycles to chariots, musical instruments, and rooms full of unusual collections. There is also a lace-making exhibition.

 Stanway is a treasure house of ancient buildings. Stanway House, now occasionally open to the public, built by the Tracy family in the mid-seventeenth century, had, as a later resident Thomas Dover, grandson of the Robert of Dover's Hill, the inventor of mercury-based medicine and a privateer who rescued Alexander Selkirk — the real Robinson Crusoe — from his desert island. The gateway to the house is oddly positioned between a high wall and the church, and its elaborate design does not fit well with the simple dignity of the church. The village also has a

massive tithe barn and a cricket pavilion set up, in typical fashion, on staddle stones, a local form of damp course. At Didbrook, the church is of considerable interest, rebuilt in 1475, following, it is said, the massacre of refugees from the Battle of Tewkesbury in the earlier church. The door is original and still shows the marks of bullets. This act was seen as a desecration and the older church was demolished. The village also contains a noteworthy pair of cottages that show at one end the 'cruck' method of construction, an external inverted V of substantial timbers to hold up the roof.

Finally, **Stanton**, perhaps the best of the villages, has a superb situation and a single street full of individual Cotswold-stone cottages and houses. This is truly a place to savour both the warm colouring of the buildings and a quiet Cotswold village with its back-drop of wooded hills.

To the east of these spring line

21

Timber-framed house at Stanton

villages, the Cotswolds seem to point a finger towards the Malverns and Wales. Alderton Hill and Dumbleton Hill, reaching about 650ft are quite low in comparison with the escarpment at this point, but the great mass of Bredon Hill, a true outlier, reaches almost 1,000ft. The first two hills, really twin summits on a single stone mass, are ringed by a series of villages. **Toddington** is only two miles from Stanway. The main A438 runs by it and appears to touch it, but the true centre is tucked away in a valley to the side. It has a collection of fine houses, and a beautiful manor set in nearly 500 acres of excellent parkland. Its fine church has a spire: surviving account books show it was erected for just £4,400 in the late nineteenth century. It was built by the Tracy family, one of whose early members, William de Tracy, was among the four knights who murdered Thomas à Becket. Memorials to the family, who are descended from King Ethelred the Unready, can be seen inside. Next to the church are the ruins of the Tracys' original seventeenth-century manor house, now sadly ruined and dangerous.

North of Toddington is **Wormington**, on the very edge of the Cotswold AONB, where, in the church, is one of Britain's most outstanding Christian treasures, a very rare Saxon crucifix, probably one thousand years old. It may be a relic of Winchcombe Abbey. The

stream that flows past the village, the River Isbourne, flows to Winchcombe. On either side of the hill are **Alderton** and **Dumbleton**, two small villages whose fine views of the Cotswold edge can be enhanced by climbing the hill along the path from Alderton, or the track from Dumbleton, the two routes meeting at Hill Farm. The actual summit of the two hills, named from the villages themselves, are wooded, the woods being privately owned. Since the triangulation station that stands on a third peak is also on private land, this walk has no firm objective in terms of a view point, but the views to the edge and to the Evesham and Severn Vales more than make up for this shortcoming.

Beyond Dumbleton/Alderton hill the Carrant Brook flows down to Tewkesbury, the last part of its course forming the border between Worcestershire and Gloucestershire. It runs through **Beckford**, where there was an Augustinian monastery in the early twelfth century on the present site of Beckford House. The stream itself was used to power mills, and a mill where visitors can watch the hand printing of silk still exists.

Beyond Beckford is **Bredon Hill**, looking 'like a stranded whale'. Because of its position, standing alone, it collects the weather and is used locally as a barometer —

W
2½m
1h
o
*

When Bredon Hill puts on its hat
ye men of the Vale beware of that
when Bredon Hill doth clear appear
ye men of the Vale have naught to fear.

The hill can be ascended by very many
paths, from each of the villages that ring
its base. The mileage given here is for an
average ascent and descent of the hill, or
on a traverse. The summit area of the
hill has many interesting spots. The
tower is Parsons Folly, built in the
eighteenth century by a gentleman of
that name from Kemerton, and is an
ideal shelter. It stands within the
ramparts of an Iron Age hillfort, which,
when excavated, revealed the mutilated
bodies of fifty men who, it is assumed,
were the defenders of the fort when the
last battle was fought there. The bodies
were not buried, but were left where they
fell and gradually overlaid with wind-
blown soil as the fort fell into disrepair.
Also within the ramparts is the Banbury
Stone. It has been considered to be either
a sacrificial stone for the Druids or a
Roman altar. At 14ft high and nearly
60ft round, it is unlikely to have been
brought here, and is, indeed, a natural
outcrop. The Cotswolds abound with
single stones, some natural, some not,
and all seem to have been considered
supernatural at some stage. It has long
been held that this stone descends the
hill to drink at the Avon each time it
hears a church clock strike twelve.

To the south of the hill is **Overbury**,
perhaps the prettiest village in
Worcestershire. The number of half-
timbered houses shows clearly that the
village is at the limit of the Cotswolds,
but there are fine stone buildings as well,
particularly Overbury Court, a largely
eighteenth-century house.

At **Kemerton**, to the west, there is the
tomb of a man killed in the Charge of
the Light Brigade. Also here, at The
Priory, is a beautiful, large, garden with
borders laid out for colour, and a good
sunken garden. On the nearby hill above
Westmancote are two more natural rock

PLACES OF INTEREST AROUND
BREDON HILL

Bredon Springs, Ashton-under-Hill
Large minimum-labour garden.
Partly wild, but with good plant
collections.

Beckford Silk Mill
Visitors may watch the handprinting
of silk

Bredon Tithe Barn
Fine fourteenth-century barn

**Banbury Stone and King and Queen
Stones, Bredon Hill**
'Supernatural' stones

The Priory, Kemerton
Large garden with colour group
borders. Sunken garden and unusual
plant collections

King and Queen Stones, Bredon Hill

23

Bredon Hill tithe barn

outcrops imbued with supernatural powers. These are called the King and Queen, and to pass between the two was considered a cure for all ills. Until quite recently — if indeed the custom has stopped — children were passed between the stones to ensure their good health.

Next is **Bredon** village itself. This has a fine tithe barn, one of the best of its kind, dating from the fourteenth century, and now in the care of National Trust. Here also came Bishop Prideaux when sacked from Worcester by Cromwell. He lived here in poverty on a miserly pension and survived only by selling his personal effects. Once, when asked how he was faring he replied: 'never better in my life, only I have too great a stomach. . . I have eaten a great library, a great deal of linen, much of my brass, some of my pewter and now I am come to eat my iron and what will come next I know not'.

From Bredon one can walk around the base of the hill to **Great Comberton**, passing Woollas Hall, a fine early seventeenth-century gabled mansion.

The return can be made over the hill. Great Comberton itself is another mainly half-timbered village, which has two good dovecotes, one containing 1,425 nest holes, the largest number of any such building in England. The village also contains many thatched houses, and is surrounded by orchards — it is clear we are leaving Cotswold country for the Vale of Evesham.

Elmley Castle, to the east of Comberton, once had a moment of glory when Elizabeth I stayed here. She did not stay at the castle itself: although slight ruins now remain, the Norman castle had been destroyed by Henry VII. She was on her way back to London, and further along the route of the county border near Ashton-under-Hill she stopped to thank the Sheriff of Worcestershire for his hospitality, although it is not known where she stayed. She also commanded him to commend her 'heartilly' to the Bailiffs of Worcester itself. This was probably because she had just borrowed £200 from them, money she never returned,

24

and probably never intended to. At **Ashton-under-Hill** is Bredon Springs, an interesting garden, maintained at a minimum level and mainly wild.

To the south of Bredon is **Tewkesbury**, just outside the AONB, but not to be missed. The town is distinctly non-Cotswold, the older buildings being almost entirely half-timbered, in keeping with the upper reaches of the River Severn, and with the Vale of Evesham from Pershore to Stratford. The Avon, which flows through the Evesham Vale between those two towns joins the Severn at Tewkesbury. But even though it lacks the architecture and stone of the Cotswolds, it is a Gloucestershire town and a place of considerable interest.

Tewkesbury Abbey is one of the largest churches in Britain, and also one of the best; it has some remains of a Benedictine Monastery, and contains some very fine Norman work. Some of the memorial tombs are very old and considered to be the finest of their type. On a calm day the abbey seems a tranquil place, but it was not always so.

PLACES OF INTEREST AROUND TEWKESBURY

Dowty Railway Society, Ashchurch
Static display of vintage rail vehicles including fine GWR collection

John Moore Museum, Tewkesbury
Natural history collection, including audio-visual display. Rural history collection with old photographs. Occasional exhibitions

Little Museum, Tewkesbury
Cottage built in 1450 and now restored as a medieval merchant's house

Town Museum, Tewkesbury
Collection on the history of the town, including model of the Battle of Tewkesbury

---

Tewkesbury

On 14 May 1471, survivors of a battle at Bloody Meadow, south of the abbey beside the A38, sought shelter inside it. The battle had ended with the defeat of the Lancastrians by the Yorkists, who then proceeded to massacre the defeated army. The Duke of Somerset and many knights fled there, although their leader Prince Edward was already dead. There is a legend that the monks at the abbey broke up the fighting that took place in the church itself. Many knights received sanctuary, but it was short lived; they were dragged from the church the following day and executed at the town cross.

Any visitor who walks around the town will be well rewarded. The Avon at Mill Bank and Abbey Mill is as picturesque as anywhere on its course and almost all the older houses in the old town have historical associations. In Church Street, in a row of fifteenth-century cottages, is the John Moore Museum containing exhibits collected by (or related to) this local novelist. There are two further museums in the town; the Little Museum (also in Church Street) which is a mid-fifteenth-century house restored to its original medieval state, and the Town Museum in Barton Street which contains many items on the history of the town, including a model of the battle. A mile to the west at Ashchurch is the collection of vintage rail carriages of the Dowty Railway Society.

2 The North-Eastern Edge

The north-eastern Cotswold villages differ little in character from those of the north-western edge. There are warm, stone villages nestling beneath tree-clad hills; here the hill is not the edge of the escarpment, but the side of a valley cut deep into the limestone. The north-eastern area, however, is also true high wold, bleak and free of woodland. Indeed the town of Stow is rightly 'on-the-Wold', having been built in an exposed position on the highest land. A further effect of this uniformly high wold is the limitation of the view. It does not extend across to the Welsh hills, but it is an equally inspiring vista of rolling wold-land.

Moreton-in-Marsh is the principal town, not only of this section of the Cotswolds, but of the entire northern area. The name is something of a misnomer, as it is doubtful whether the area around the town was ever marshland. It is more likely that 'marsh' is a corruption of 'merche' or 'march', the ancient name for a boundary. To support this theory, there is, about two miles east of the town on the A44 to Chipping Norton, a Four-Shires Stone, which formerly marked the boundary of the counties of Gloucestershire, Oxfordshire, Warwickshire and Worcestershire. Following the redrawing of county boundaries in 1928 however there are now only three county boundaries meeting at the stone, the county of Worcester (and Hereford) having withdrawn about ten miles north-west.

The Foss Way, an important road in Roman times, was the effective western boundary of Roman Britain for some time, as the Romans attempted to subdue the Silurian tribesmen to the west of the River Severn. Moreton straddles the Foss Way (now the main A429) in elegant fashion; the broad, tree-lined High Street with its occasional wide, grassed, verges being a perfect foreground for the rows of late-eighteenth- and early nineteenth-century houses. The majority of these houses were built when the town was an important coaching stage, and also the centre of a linen weaving industry. Linen weaving grew up after the decline of the woollen industry, first using locally grown flax and then imported material.

Four-Shires Stone

Chastleton House
Jacobean manor house with considerable amount of original decor and furniture. Fine long gallery

Sezincote Gardens
Oriental garden around Indian style house. Many interesting features including water garden

Batsford Park Arboretum

Curfew Tower, Moreton-in-Marsh
Bell dates from the seventeenth century

Four-Shires Stone
Ancient county boundary stone

Rollright Stones
Three groups of standing stones, the remains of a long barrow and stone circle

T
1m
ooo
*

The town is worth exploring in detail as it is a fine example of a late Cotswold market town. The church, St David's, is mid-nineteenth century, though it may incorporate very much earlier work. It used to contain perhaps the most amusing epitaph in the Cotswolds:

Here lie the bones of Richard Lawton
whose death, alas, was strangeley brought on,
trying one day his corns to mow off
the razor slipped, and cut his toe off

West of the church the old parsonage is of comparable age, although tiled in Welsh slate rather than the local stone. At the corner of Church Street and High Street is the Manor House Hotel, one of the older houses in the town, dating from the mid-seventeenth century. This provides a direct comparison with Chipping Campden, which has many houses of considerably greater age. The influence of Moreton's linen industry is clearly visible in the number of later houses.

The Manor House is said to be haunted. Further along High Street is the White Hart Hotel where Charles I is said to have spent a night in the summer of 1644 during the Civil War, although an inscription suggests a construction date of 1782! The Curfew Tower, on the corner of Oxford Street, is definitely sixteenth century and is the oldest

building in the town. The tower still contains the last curfew bell, dated 1633, which was rung daily until the mid-nineteenth century and even later to call the local fire brigade. High Street is dominated by the imposing lines of Redesdale Hall, in the middle of the old broad road. The building is also known as Market Hall, a reminder that this has long been the local market town, a tradition maintained by a weekly market held on Tuesdays, with stalls laid out along the west side of the High Street. Finally Moreton Station, opened in 1843, a living museum of early railway history, provides a profitable visit for those interested in the development of the British railway system.

Close to Moreton, and the northern extremity of the Cotswolds, are two charming villages — Bourton-on-the-Hill and Blockley, typical of this part of the Cotswolds; with Blockley nestling in a secluded valley, while Bourton, nearly two hundred feet higher, appears set out in open wold. From Moreton a single walk takes in a number of places of interest. The walk goes by fields to Batsford Park entrance, by lane to Bourton-on-the-Hill; southward by path to Sezincote Park, passing close to the house itself, and from the far side of the park a track goes back towards Moreton, finally becoming a meandering path across farmland.

W
6½
2¼
oo
*

28

   The house at Batsford Park was built
in the late nineteenth century, the park
having been landscaped by Lord
Redesdale a little earlier. Redesdale was
the British Ambassador to Japan
around 1850 and imported many
oriental ideas as well as statues and
plants. A bronze Buddha, some deer and
dolphins were all brought back from
Japan and there is a replica of a Chinese
temple. The park is now an arboretum
with fine collections of trees and shrubs.
The higher areas of the park offer fine
views of the Evenlode Valley. As well as
the arboretum there is a garden centre
which sells many of the trees and shrubs
that grow there.
   Bourton was also once 'on-the-
Merche', as was Moreton, but although

it is now 'on-the-Hill', it is in fact just
below the level of the high wolds; the
village straddles the A 44 as it descends
towards Moreton. It is an unlikely site
for a village, but still excellent. The
visitor arriving from Moreton passes, at
the base of the hill, Bourton House,
which still contains some sixteenth-
century work and has a superb tithe
barn, the largest in the area, inscribed
'R. P. 1570'. R. P. is for Richard Palmer,
and is a link with a murder that, in its
day, was as famous as the Chipping
Campden wonder. Palmer was, by
marriage, connected to the remarkable
Overbury family. Sir Thomas Overbury
wrote the first detailed account of the
Campden Wonder, but before that, in
1613, an earlier Thomas Overbury was

29

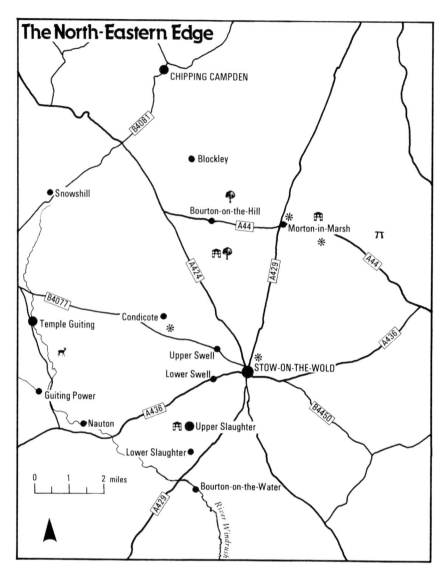

The North-Eastern Edge

CHIPPING CAMPDEN

B4081

Blockley

Snowshill

Bourton-on-the-Hill

A44

Morton-in-Marsh

A424

A429

A44

B4077

Condicote

Temple Guiting

Upper Swell

Lower Swell

STOW-ON-THE-WOLD

A436

Guiting Power

A436

B4450

Nauton

Upper Slaughter

Lower Slaughter

0   1   2 miles

Bourton-on-the-Water

A429

River Windrush

the victim of a real and very unpleasant murder. Thomas opposed the marriage of his friend, and a favourite of James I, Robert Carr, to Frances Howard, Lady Essex, not least because she was already married. He reputedly told Lady Essex that she 'might do for a mistress, but not for a wife'. To silence him, Lady Essex had him wrongfully imprisoned in the Tower where he was poisoned with laced cakes. The cakes contained 'arsenic, aqua fortis, mercury, powder of diamonds, lapis costitus, great spiders and cantharides'. The diamonds were certainly an expensive gesture and one can only hope that the spiders were dead. The combination did not kill Sir Thomas quickly. Indeed he was in great agony for months and was reduced to a skeleton, his doctor maintaining that his illness was due to natural causes. Eventually it was decided that he was to be released, and a large dose of a 'corrosive' substance was administered as a *coup de grâce*. Some three years later the young apothecary who had obtained the poison confessed, and Lady Essex, now Carr's wife, Carr himself and several others were committed to the Tower. The Carrs, saved by their rank, were released after five years, but several of their accomplices were hanged. Local opinion was, not surprisingly, rather hard on Lady Essex, and the story provided local entertainment for a long time.

 South of Bourton-on-the-Hill is **Sezincote**, famous for its house and garden. The house was remodelled in the early eighteenth century by Sir Charles Cockerell whose wealth derived from his work with the East India Company. He obviously enjoyed the East, and had the house constructed in Indian style with oriental gardens. The architects for the house and garden were Daniell and Repton, assisted by Cockerell's brother. The park is clearly the work of a great British eccentric, and Sir Charles obviously had a good pedigree for the task, his parents having christened his brother Samuel Pepys Cockerell. In its day the park was a very bold venture and impressed the Prince Regent so much during a visit in 1807 that he decided to use a similar but more subdued design for his own planned extravaganza, the Brighton Pavilion. There is a profusion of exotic trees, and one should not miss the bridge over the landscaped valley north of the house, and the Wellington Memorial, which serves also as a chimney for the greenhouse heating system.

Those who enjoy walking along English country lanes can extend a visit to Batsford Park by visiting Batsford village and walking down to **Aston Magna**. This is a pleasant village grouped around a green; it still has the base of its medieval village cross. Beyond Aston is **Draycott**, another small

village from which the walker can return directly by fields to Batsford, or continue to Blockley before returning.

Blockley itself is well worth a visit. It is a delightful place, perhaps the finest, and most unspoilt, of the larger Cotswold villages. Like many other Cotswold communities it suffered from the decline of the woollen industry, which affected all the northern towns and villages, alleviated in its case by the continued production from its eight silk mills. Because of them it has survived remarkably well; the old workhouse, in the High Street, has even been converted into an antique shop; some of the old mills have been similarly converted; many of the houses on Blockley Brook at the southern end of the village were mills in the sixteenth and seventeenth century. The village also possesses a fine collection of genuinely ancient inns, now selling real ale. The history of the village during the last 300 years has been closely linked to that of the Northwick family who built nearby Northwick Park and its mansions. Particularly noteworthy was John Rushout, the second Lord Northwick who once sailed with Lord Nelson, Sir William and Lady Hamilton. He constructed the Five Mile Drive which is such a feature of the A44 above Blockley, and also landscaped the valley at the south end of the village now known as Dovedale, to the fascination and confusion of lovers of the Peak District.

From the end of Blockley High Street, which actually leads nowhere, the visitor can follow a track through Dovedale to Bourton Woods and through them to the Five Mile Drive. Apart from this one track on the southern side, the woods are private, though access is allowed at most times. Within, there is excellent woodland walking.

South of Sezincote is a trio of picturesque villages on the high wold, snatching what cover they can from the folding of the landscape. **Longborough** has a church with Norman doorways; it contains both a monumental bust of Sir

Charles Cockerell of Sezincote Park, and a fine effigy in armour that dates from the early fourteenth century. Nearby is **Condicote**. *The Victoria County History of Gloucestershire* notes that 'except that the land was sometimes owned by important people, Condicote has no associations with figures or events of national fame or notoriety. Its remoteness and its physical condition are the kind to have made the life of the community as uneventful as it is austere'! Be that as it may, the village has much of interest. Its church contains a large amount of Norman work; and a group of beautiful eighteenth-century Cotswold farmhouses surround an old village green that still has its ancient cross. The cross could be 600 years old, but is modern in comparison with the site now exposed on the eastern side of the village. This site is believed to be a neolithic ceremonial, or 'henge', site, and as such, pre-dates the cross by several thousand years. Condicote Lane, the Roman Ryknield Street runs through the village down towards the Foss Way at Stow. This can be followed over the local high point, at around 880ft, returning by lanes to the village. This is a most interesting walk following in the steps of Romans and giving a very good view of the high wold. This area, to the west of Condicote, is a superb expanse of enclosed and cultivated wold. Cleeve Common gives a good impression of how the original wolds must have

W
4m
1½h
ooo
*

looked, but this area, between Condicote and the Guitings, is an excellent example of the more modern landscape.

Donnington is the third of the villages, and is famous as the place of the surrender of Lord Astley and his army in 1646 in the final battle of the first Civil War. Astley is famous for the couplet:

Lord I shall be verie busie this day
I may forget Thee, but doe not Thou
forget me

coined before the Battle of Newbury. Astley had reached Stow on his way to join the King at Oxford. History records his final act of surrender after the battle, painting a sorry picture of an old and tired soldier — 'taken captive and wearyed in his fight, and being ancient — for old age's silver haires had quite covered over his head and beard'. His 'soldiers brought him a Drum to sit and rest himselfe upon' and he told them and his captors to 'sit downe and play, for you have done all your worke' adding, prophetically, to the Parliamentarians, 'if you fall not out among yourselves'.

On a more cheerful note there is, between the villages of Condicote and Donnington, a brewery that produces real ale. The site, on a long lake, appears most incongruous in the wold land, but is the result of the extension of an old mill pond. The old mill-wheel still helps to power the brewery, which is housed in an old mill building with a dovecote in

Cotswold Farm Park

Chipping Campden almshouses

Hidcote Manor gardens

Snowshill

Moreton-in-Marsh

Naunton

one wall. The brewery grows its own barley and so is completely self-contained; it produces beer that, when bottled, requires skilful pouring, as it also contains old-fashioned sediment. Near the brewery is Donnington Fish Farm, a very modern trout farm based in a beautiful seventeenth-century barn. All stages in the life of the trout can be seen, and a shop on the premises sells fresh and smoked trout, and salmon in season.

At Bemborough Farm is the Cotswold Farm Park which concentrates on the breeding of ancient species of domesticated animals. The co-director of the park was a founder of the Rare Breeds Survival Trust, and the animals on show are part of the most comprehensive collection of breeds in the trust. Soay sheep, one of the oldest breeds, live on seaweed on the islands of St Kilda, and Manx Loghtan sheep are of Viking origin and have four horns. The pigs include the beautifully coloured Tamworth Gingers and the hardy, and local, Gloucester Old Spot; these do not need cover, and can survive on fallen apples. There are goats and geese, cattle and chickens, but pride of place must go to the famous local breeds. Firstly there are genuine Cotswold sheep, with the traditional fringe, giving them a look more akin to Old English Sheepdogs than Old English sheep; there are also the Old Gloucester cattle, perhaps now the rarest breed in Britain, whose milk made the original Double Gloucester cheese. In addition to the penned animals there is a pets' corner with sheep, goats and pigs to feed, rides in an ox-drawn cart and barns containing educational exhibits, souvenirs and refreshments. The large car-parking field is ideal for picnics and those interested in the workings of a modern farm can take the Bemborough Farm Trail which meanders across the wolds with explanatory boards at strategic points.

South of the Farm Park is **Naunton**, on the River Windrush. This village, which has an excellent church containing some Saxon features, a fine gabled dovecote with over a thousand nest holes and is on the Windrush, could be perfect. But it is just a little too long,

33

and appears to straggle. Perhaps the view from the A436 south of, and above, the village, where too much of the village can be seen, betrays it, for the limited aspect from the northern approach by country lanes is much more pleasant. The view from the south, with the church and a cluster of cottages close to it, against a backdrop of wold, is well-known.

Naunton, as with all villages close to Stow, shows evidence of the Civil War. As if to represent the feelings of the majority of the ordinary people at that time who waved Parliamentarian and Royalist flags with equal vigour at various times, the town's evidence is double-headed. In St Andrew's church there is a marble memorial to Ambrose Oldys recording that he was 'barbarously murdered by ye rebells' in 1645 after having 'escaped many and eminent dangers in battles for ye honour and service of his King'. By contrast, further down the Windrush is Cromwell House built before the war, but renamed by the Aylworth family in honour of the Protector. Indeed it was Richard Aylworth who stopped the King's army at Stow in 1644. The Aylworths are also commemorated at a hamlet of that name which can be reached by a path across the wold, and along a tributary stream of the Windrush, from the A436 above Naunton, returning to there by country lanes. The hamlet was part of a larger estate that extended over much of the land in this area south of the Windrush.

An attraction of Naunton is the Windrush, and the walk from Harford Bridge to the Foss Bridge near Bourton-on-the-Water is as delightful as any of the 'softer' river valleys to the south. The route is straightforward enough, leaving the minor road from Harford Bridge just after crossing the Windrush. From there the route follows the river as it meanders gently towards Foss Bridge. At the Foss Bridge end an old, now trackless, railway embankment is crossed, and the walker can use an old railway bridge to cross the river, as both banks of the river

have pathways. This walk can, of course, be started from Naunton for ease of parking. The quoted mileage is for the *single* bridge to bridge route.

Taking the A436 from Harford Bridge towards Stow the traveller drops down to cross the Eye valley. Here, to the south of the road, are the villages of Upper and Lower Slaughter, pictures of which have, rightly, adorned almost every book ever compiled on the beauties of the Cotswolds. Massingham, the writer on the English countryside, maintained that the two villages, together with the two Swells, a little closer to Stow 'perfectly exemplify, as no other group quite does, the unique and local genius of the Cotswold style'. Massingham preferred the Slaughters and particularly Upper Slaughter. Even a car driving through the village seems to disturb the timelessness of the cottages grouped around the church and manor. From the Eye Bridge on the A436 a walk of only one and a half miles is needed to reach both villages, and, a further half mile beyond the second, the A429 is reached. For those who have to make the visit by car, the road about one and half miles north of Harford Bridge, dropping down the side of the valley and giving superb views of both Slaughters in the wooded valley floor, should be used.

The River Eye is known in its two-mile section between the main roads as the Slaughterbrook. The name Slaughter has no evil connections, as it derives from the Saxon for either 'the place of the Sloe trees' or 'the place of the pools'. Only the latter is now appropriate. **Upper Slaughter** is so rich in interest and beauty that the traveller should wander at will, but he should not miss the ford, which is still used, nor the farms, cottages and superb trees gathered around it. There is a fine dovecote up-river of the ford. The church has been 'modernised' several times, not always successfully, but is still worthy of note. One rector was the Rev F. E. Witts who wrote *The Diary of a Cotswold Parson*.

W
2½m
1h
o
*

V
3m
1h
ooo
*

V
2m
¾h
ooo
*

Upper Slaughter

Lower Slaughter

35

At the true village centre there is a small reminder of the green and, beyond, two manors. One is the original manor house, a largely Elizabethan house built on earlier foundations. It has been described as the most beautiful domestic house in the Cotswolds, with its row of dormer windows and Jacobean doorway. The other manor was 'The Manor': it was the old parsonage but took a new name in the nineteenth century when the rector became Lord of the Manor. It is now a hotel.

Lower Slaughter also has a ford, but here the brook follows the road closely for much further, the village being grouped around it. One added advantage of the brook is that one side of it allows a car-free walk past excellent stone cottages. At one end of the village is the old mill, complete with waterwheel. The mill has a brick chimney which, strangely, seems in no way incongruous. At the other end of

The Mill, Lower Slaughter

the village opposite the Manor House is a tree-sheltered green beside the brook. Beside the Manor is a sixteenth-century dovecote, one of the largest in Gloucestershire.

In the valley of the Dikler, a stream that, like the Eye, flows to Bourton-on-the-Water, are the Swells, named from a shortening of 'Our Lady's Well'. **Upper Swell** is only a half mile south of the Donnington brewery. As car parking is banned on the narrow road through the village the interested traveller must walk from lay-bys on the B4077. Those walking from the direction of Stow reach a right-angled bridge with excellent views of the mill and mill-pond, before turning into the village itself. The round trip from here is best accomplished by going along the lane from Upper to Lower Swell, returning by track and path along the Dikler. **Lower Swell** is, in fact, away from the river and seems to suffer as a result. It has some interesting corners, however; the visitor who has been to Sezincote will undoubtedly have a sense of *déjà vu* when he sees Spa Cottages. To the west of the villages are several long barrows and other reminders of prehistory. The solitary, enigmatic Hoar Stone, about half a mile south-west of Lower Swell, is also thought to be the remnant of a long barrow.

Visits to the Slaughters and the Swells inevitably lead the traveller to **Stow-on-the-Wold**. This delightful market town is, with Moreton, perhaps the best known of the small Cotswold towns. The addition to the name is as recent as the sixteenth century, the town having been previously called Stow St Edward. The religious name was given by the Abbot of Evesham who sited the town here at the crossing of many major roads at about 800ft with no sheltering hill on any side. The locals say it has no earth, fire or water, but plenty of air, and a local couplet maintains:

Stow-on-the-Wold
where the wind blows cold

V
2m
¾h
oo
*

When the Cotswolds became rich during the wool boom, Stow, with its two annual fairs, was a centre of considerable importance. Daniel Defoe, during his journey through the area, recorded that at one fair over 20,000 sheep were sold, and that such huge numbers were not uncommon. The size of the market place, around which the town is built, is indicative of these fairs, at which both sheep and horses were sold. Such was their importance that they became a unit of time and certainty — 'three years next fair' and 'as sure as the fair'.

The town church is dedicated to St Edward; its continued existence is remarkable when one recalls that after the Civil War battle at Donnington in 1646, in which a large Royalist army was totally defeated, prisoners were incarcerated in it. The conditions of their imprisonment were, to say the least, primitive and their behaviour was, not surprisingly in view of the executions

Lower Swell

PLACES OF INTEREST AROUND STOW-ON-THE-WOLD

Upper Slaughter Manor
Beautiful Elizabethan house. Some later work is equally fine. Set in one of the most picturesque Cotswold villages.

Cotswold Farm Park
The most comprehensive collection of rare breeds of domesticated farm animals in Britain. Includes cows, pigs, sheep, goats and poultry. Pets' corner, picnic area and exhibition centre

Trout Farm, Donnington
Trout Farm in a seventeenth-century barn. Trout and salmon on sale.

Bemborough Farm Trail
Trail through a modern farm. Same site as Cotswold Farm Park

Town Stocks, Stow-on-the-Wold

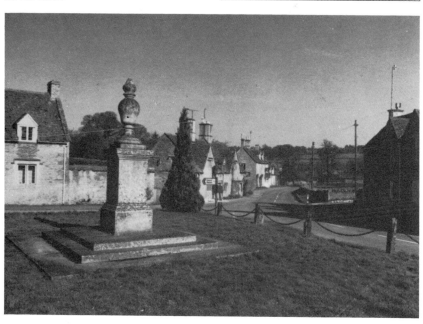

Stow-on-the-Wold

that were frequently carried out on prisoners at that time, appalling. After this use as a prison, the church was declared ruined. Fortunately in the latter part of the seventeenth century it was restored, although further major work was required 200 years later. Despite numerous deaths, the churchyard contains only one, marked, grave of a soldier from the battle or its aftermath — that of Capt Keyte.

The church is on the west side of the market square. Walking around the square, and the rest of the town, the visitor is faced with an elegant array of Cotswold town houses. St Edward's Hall, now the County Library, is Victorian, and dominates the centre of the square, and St Edward's House is perhaps the best of the eighteenth-century houses. At one end is the town cross, of which only the base is ancient; at the other are the original town stocks.

Despite the association of Stow with the Foss Way, and the references to the road in several house and hotel names, the Way does not actually pass through the town, which is about 1 mile north.

But it does pass through Maugersbury, an excellent village, just a little way from the town. Just before Maugersbury the Way passes yet another reminder, in name, of the town's ecclesiastical beginnings — St Edward's Well — an artificial pond and stream that marked one extreme of a nineteenth century pleasure garden designed in Romantic style. Stow has had some remarkable, or at least strange, inhabitants. Richard Enoch built a tower on the Oddington road and there he planted what was, he claimed, the one grain of corn that was buried with an Egyptian. Although it was about 2,500 years old, it grew fifteen stems and yielded over 1,600 grains — each counted by Enoch.

Five miles north-east of Stow is Chastleton House, a Jacobean manor built around the turn of the seventeenth century on land bought from Robert Catesby, a Gunpowder Plotter. The house is more famous for its interior than its exterior, being lavishly furnished in true period style. Its very fine panelling contains a secret chamber which was used to good effect in 1651 by

T
1m
oo
**

38

The Stocks, Stow-on-the-Wold

a member of the family, fleeing from the Battle of Worcester. His pursuers evidently thought he was the king himself and, having failed to find him, they decided to spend the night in the room that contained the chamber! Luckily the man had a brave wife who drugged the soldiers with laudanum, thus giving her husband time to escape. A poignant relic of the earlier phase of the Civil War is the Bible carried by Charles I to the scaffold. The gardens are as great an attraction as the house; they include work from the seventeenth and eighteenth centuries, and a fine topiary.

Some 4 miles further east from Chastleton are the prehistoric Rollright Stones. There are three monuments on an extended site: a stone circle, 100ft across with seventy stones known as the King's Men; a solitary stone — the King; and a group of five stones — the Whispering Knights. In truth they are the remains of a long barrow and ceremonial circle about 4,000 years old, but local legend has it that they were a boastful king, and his followers, turned to stone by a local witch. The stones were long held in awe by the locals, and there is a story that a farmer, ignoring superstitions, tried to move one away. His team of horses toiled all day but dragged it only a few yards. Convinced of the stone's power, he decided to restore it to its original position, a feat accomplished by one horse, with ease.

39

3 The Area Around Cheltenham

This area of the Cotswolds comprises Cheltenham, the escarpment north of Cheltenham and a slice of high wold across to the A429. It contains an excellent cross-section of the landscapes that make up the Cotswolds.

Cheltenham is now a spacious and splendid town; until the latter part of the eighteenth century it was just a small village, tucked underneath the Cotswold edge, on the road between the important towns of Gloucester and Winchcombe. Henry VIII did endow a grammar school in the village, but it seems likely that the importance of the village was

due more to its proximity to Gloucester and a Royal Manor, than to its own merits. The village became important following the Civil War when the area from Cheltenham to Winchcombe became well-known for growing tobacco. It was first planted by William Stratford near Winchcombe, and when it proved successful, the fields from there to Cheltenham were rapidly taken over for its production. Indeed there were isolated fields of tobacco as far south as Bristol. The crop was soon worth the remarkable sum of £1,500 a year. But the Government became fearful that this

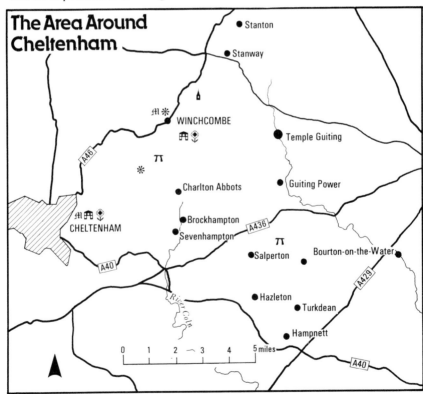

The Area Around Cheltenham

Stanton
Stanway
WINCHCOMBE
Temple Guiting
Charlton Abbots
Guiting Power
CHELTENHAM
Brockhampton
Sevenhampton
Salperton
Bourton-on-the-Water
Hazleton
Turkdean
Hampnett

0 1 2 3 4 5 miles

A46
A40
A436
A429
A40

River Coln

new, home-produced crop would harm
the prosperity of the new colonies in
America, especially Virginia, which were
almost entirely dependent on their
tobacco crop, and so made its
cultivation illegal here. The decision was
not popular and a series of pro-tobacco
propaganda pamphlets was issued. The
best of these was *Henry Hangman's
Horror, or Gloucestershire's request to
the smokers and tobacconists of London.*
This was a nice piece of black humour;
Hangman's trade had declined locally
since the lawful growing of tobacco had
become widespread, and the real aim of
the ban was to produce a crime wave
and increase in executions. The
propaganda was unsuccessful, however,
and illicit growing was stamped on hard.
Riots were frequent as soldiers arrived to
destroy crops. The locals were referred
to as a 'rabble of men and women calling
for blood for the tobacco', and blood
they got when they attacked an army
detachment, killing men and horses.
Henry Hangman got his way and the
growing ceased. But a large field near
Bristol continued to grow the crop for a
further fifty years.

After the destruction of tobacco
growing, Winchcombe became
desperately poor, but Cheltenham's
market continued to maintain trade and
some prosperity in the town. In 1716 a
Quaker farmer, William Mason,
wondered why flocks of pigeons
gathered to feed in one of his fields. On
investigation he found that the birds
were pecking at salt crystallizing near a
spring in the field. Cheltenham was close
enough to Bath and Clifton for Mason
to realise that if this water were
drinkable he could have a valuable asset.
He had it analysed, and, after
confirmation that it was pure mineral
water, he had a locked shed erected over
the spring, surrounded with a stout
fence. Water was bottled and sold, some
being sent as far as London. Mason
however was a man of only limited
ambition for when his daughter and son-
in-law, Capt Henry Skillicorne, a retired

PLACES OF INTEREST AROUND
CHELTENHAM

Cheltenham College
Fine chapel and college buildings
with much original work

Pittville Pump Room, Cheltenham
Regency mansion in large park.
Display of costume and jewellery
from the eighteenth to twentieth
centuries

**Gustav Holst Birthplace Museum
Cheltenham**
Collection of Holst memorabilia
set in reconstructed Victorian
house. Also a collection of
eighteenth and nineteenth century
musical instruments.

**Town Museum and Art Gallery,
Cheltenham**
Collections of paintings, pottery
and metalwork. Displays of local
archaeology and history.
Collection of Edward Wilson
memorabilia

merchant seaman, inherited the land in
1738, the spring was 'open and exposed
to the weather'. But Skillicorne was a
good business man: Cheltenham Spa
was born. The early history of the spring
in the early eighteenth century may be
read on Skillicorne's 587 word epitaph
— the longest in Britain — in the parish
church.

Skillicorne, after building four brick
arches over the spring, dug out the
spring to produce a well and installed a
pump. A road was then made to the well
from the village. The beginnings were
small, but steady; a report in 1740 on
mineral waters in Britain stated that
those in Cheltenham were the best. It
was claimed to have 'action' without

Regency buildings, Cheltenham

'dryness, sickness, gripings or dejection of the spirit', and was effective for 'bilious conditions, obstruction of liver, spleen and perspiration, and all disorders of the *primae viae*'.

Dr Johnson came, as did Handel, but Cheltenham was off the beaten track, three days by fast coach from London, and trade slackened. After Skillicorne died the spa seemed doomed also, despite his son's efforts, but in 1788 George III visited the village to take the waters. The king with his queen and children, and the queen's lady-in-waiting Fanny Burney, stayed for a month. The construction of the elegant modern town now began, and its popularity increased. Jane Austen even deserted her beloved Bath for a few weeks; the racecourse, still famous today, was laid out; and new pump rooms were constructed.

Not everyone was impressed. William Cobbett in his *Rural Rides* in 1821 thought that Cheltenham was 'a nasty ill-looking place, half clown, half cockney', peopled with 'East India plunderers, West Indian floggers, English tax-gorgers, together with gluttons, drunkards and debauchees of all descriptions, female as well as male', here at the suggestion of 'silently laughing quacks, in the hope of getting rid of the bodily consequences of their manifold sins and iniquities'. He returned in the following year and noted with delight that building work was decreasing. It was 'the desolation of abomination. I have seldom seen anything with more heart-felt satisfaction. The whole town . . . looked delightfully dull'. He noted 'it is curious to see the names that the vermin owners have put upon the houses there'. The towns-people were not amused, and burned him in effigy, but the social bubble was indeed bursting. The socialites and water-takers departed, and left Cheltenham almost as we find it today.

Regency Cheltenham is best seen by taking the leisurely promenade for which it was constructed. To prove the point 'The Promenade' leads into the new town centre from the Lansdown/Montpellier area. The walk should start from Montpellier Gardens: Lansdown Place, behind, was constructed in the early nineteenth century, about 60 years after Bath's Royal Crescent. The difference is quite striking; the buildings here seem altogether more modern, less spacious and elegant. Cheltenham was indeed laid out on a grand scale and the gardens at Montpellier are a delight.

Montpellier itself, the streets that border the gardens, was built by the architect, John Papworth, who designed Lansdown Place. The Montpellier Arcade and Rotunda (now Lloyds Bank) have more character. The Rotunda itself, which is distinctively different from anything else in the area, was the pump room of Montpellier Spa. At the east end of Montpellier is the Ladies College for which Cheltenham is

famous. The college was founded in 1853 and was a very bold venture for the period.

From Montpellier the broad, beautiful, tree-lined Promenade runs towards the new town centre, where there is a statue to a famous son of Cheltenham, Dr Edward Wilson, who died with Captain Scott in the Antarctic on the successful polar expedition. The statue is actually by Scott's wife. To the right of the Promenade is the Town Hall, where some of the Festival events are held. The Hall stands in Imperial Square which has another fine garden area. Beyond the square is Trafalgar Street, where Captain Hardy lived. Those who like guided tours can arrange to join those conducted by the local tourist office.

To the north of High Street, at the end of the Promenade, is Pittville Park, where the last of the Cheltenham spas was situated. It is named after Joseph Pitt who 'used to hold gentlemen's horses for a penny, when, appearing as a sharp lad, an attorney at Cirencester

Edward Wilson's statue, The Promenade, Cheltenham

Pittville Park Gate, Cheltenham

took a fancy to him and bred him to his own business.' Pitt became a lawyer, self-taught, and used his money for land speculation, amassing a fortune with which he used to develop the park and the surrounding area. His pump room is a remarkable building being, on three sides, a copy of the Temple of Ilissus in Athens. The pump room is open to visitors and the spa water can still be taken. In Clarence Street, a little way north of the Promenade, is the museum and art gallery. Here there is a fine collection of local prints, many local exhibits, including the finds from the Belas Knap long barrow, and a collection of memorabilia of Edward Wilson. Also in Clarence Street, at number 4, is the Gustav Holst museum, the house in which Holst was born in 1847. Much of his early work was inspired by the Cotswold countryside, particularly around Bourton-on-the-Water and Wyck Rissington, where he had his first professional engagement.

About eight miles to the east of Cheltenham is a group of six small villages and hamlets set on the high wolds which capture the feel of the old Cotswolds as no other area does. They are small collections of fine stone farmhouses clustered around churches, getting what shelter they can from a protective ring of trees, and defying the winter winds that sweep across the wolds. Here it is quiet, an almost secretive quiet. The first of these villages is Cold Aston, now called **Aston Blank**, to avoid confusion with Cold Ashton further south. But the new name does not aptly describe the village, when the winter winds sweep across the wold. The grey and sturdy houses seem to have been built especially to take this weather; sturdy too, is the rugged yew in the churchyard, at least fifteen feet around its trunk.

From Aston Blank a very fine walk links five of the villages. A farm track to Turkdean is followed by a lane to

Hampnett. To shorten the walk, and not greatly detract from its beauty or interest, this section can be omitted, so reducing the walk to around seven miles. From Turkdean to Hazleton the walk follows a straightforward track, while the longer route from Hampnett follows a lane that dips sharply about half way between the villages. From Hazleton the route heads across fields towards Salperton, but before the village, turns west at the edge of Salperton Park to follow a track and path to Notgrove. From here the start is regained by paths across high flat wold.

The first village reached from Aston Blank is **Turkdean**, which is divided into two villages by an avenue of beautiful beech trees; beyond is **Hampnett**. Here there are fine views towards Northleach and its church. Hampnett's own church is interesting: a Victorian vicar attempted to recreate the feel of a medieval church by painting the wall and ceiling. The painting is a geometric pattern rather than the usual medieval scenes of saints and sinners, but the bursts of colour must be similar to the effect that the older wall painter hoped to achieve.

Westward, at **Hazleton** churchyard is a stone coffin thought to be 800 years old. The tithe barn here burnt down in 1885, a barn so big — it was reputedly the biggest ever built in Gloucestershire — that it took two weeks to burn.

Salperton, not to be confused with Sapperton further south, seems the loneliest and bleakest of all the villages. The nearby trackless railway embankment makes one feel that the village has been forgotten. Yet Salperton has as fine an early nineteenth-century house as exists in the Cotswolds, set in an equally fine park. In the churchyard is a memorial with an inscription mentioning that James Harter of the Salperton Park house died of wounds in 1917 near Jerusalem, while helping to free the Holy Land from the hand of the infidel: one of his ancestors had fought in the Crusades of the thirteenth century, for the same cause.

Nearest to Aston Blank is **Notgrove**, to the west of which is a very famous long barrow, 150ft long, now in the care of the Department of the Environment. The excavated contents of the barrow, chiefly the bones of nine persons, are now in Cheltenham museum. The village itself spreads wider than Aston Blank and is, perhaps, more picturesque because of this lack of order.

Closer to Cheltenham are villages strung out along a tributary headstream of the Coln, or the Coln itself. The first is little more than a hamlet at **Syreford** and from there a good walk by path along the stream leads to **Sevenhampton**, from where a lane or pathway (now on the other side of the river) leads on to **Brockhampton**. Each of these larger villages has a fine manor house, the latter standing in a substantial park. A return journey, doubling the stated mileage, can be made by lanes, but it is easiest to return on the outward route, using the other bank of the stream. An extention of the walk, also by pathway along the river — for about 1½ miles — can be made by passing the stream spring itself and reaching Charlton Abbots, another charming village with a good manor house.

As he continues towards Cheltenham, the visitor passes **Whittington**, where the church stands on the lawn of the old Court: around it are still the signs of an old moat — it was originally built as a fortified mansion. North from here is **Cleeve Hill**, the last unenclosed piece of high wold land left in the Cotswolds, and which at 1,075ft is also the highest point of the AONB. The summit is marked by a triangulation point which can be reached by a walk of a few yards from a car park. It is near a wall that overlooks it, as do the nearby radio masts. The land on each side slopes so gently that any one of dozens of spots could have been used to mark the summit. As a place of pilgrimage, it is disappointing and sad.

By walking from the masts along the

common, the visitor gains an idea of the original form of the wold, and has excellent views of Winchcombe and Sudeley in the valley to the north-east, and of the Malverns and Wales to the west. Since Cleeve is unenclosed there is no danger of trespass, and the walker can wander at will — but he must beware of golf balls! The most worthwhile walk, however, is to visit the Cotswold summit and then go north to follow the edge of the common with its views to Winchcombe. At the next triangulation point, to the west, a panorama dial points out the distant hills. On the summit of Cleeve Cloud, a cliff of the local limestone, is an Iron Age hillfort whose ditches have now been utilised to defend a golf green. By descending to the valley of the River Isbourne, the visitor can pass Winchcombe and arrive at Hailes

Abbey. The best way to reach this spot, and return, is by the Pilgrims Way along the quaintly named Puck Pit Lane. This route (very muddy in wet weather) is on the Cotswold Way and is well-signed.

Hailes Abbey is now administered by the National Trust. It was built around 1250 and dissolved in 1539. At the height of its prosperity it was one of the most important abbeys in England; it possessed a phial of Sacred Blood collected at the Crucifixion. The relic was mentioned by Chaucer and drew pilgrims from all over England, who paid money to be absolved of their sins in its presence. At the dissolution the relic was opened and publicly exposed as honey coloured with saffron. It was also said that the monks had obtained money from pilgrims by fraud. The glass phial was said to have been opaque on one side and clear on the other and the pilgrim was told that only those not in mortal sin could see the blood. On being shown the opaque side the fearful visitor then paid in full and 'miraculously' the blood appeared. In the museum on the site there are some of the more finely worked pieces of stone. Of the silver and other treasures, nothing remains, the abbey having been stripped of everything, including the lead roof, at its

Hailes Abbey

Winchcombe Church

dissolution. The nearby church contains some remarkable medieval wall-paintings that are being carefully restored. They depict not only the expected ecclesiastical scenes, but a hunting scene and other smaller secular pictures, including a beautiful owl.

Winchcombe is the largest town on the north-eastern edge. There was once an abbey here, but unlike Hailes, there is nothing now visible, except a cross (on private land) that marks the position of the altar. The town was a capital of Saxon Mercia and has, in St Peter's church, the stone coffins that may be those of a Mercian King, Kenulf and his son, the boy-saint Kenelm. Kenelm was murdered in Shropshire by order of his ambitious sister and his body was brought back here by monks from the abbey who had been guided to the spot by a heavenly shaft of light. His sister, stunned by the finding of the body, appeared at the window as it was being carried by, reading Psalm 108 backwards and 'at that moment her eyes, torn by divine vengeance from their hollow sockets, scattered blood

The Old Corner Cupboard Inn, Winchcombe

Winchcombe

48

upon the verse'. Until the discovery of the coffins the story was believed to be entirely legend, but the presence in the smaller coffin of not only the bones of a boy, but also a large dagger — the reputed murder weapon — has now suggested that parts of the story may be true.

As well as the church, there are other points of interest in the town. Many of its inns, particularly the George and the Corner Cupboard, are very ancient and full of character. There is a small railway museum which the enthusiast will not fail to visit. The old stocks exist, opposite the George Hotel. There is a wide variety of shops, and on the Broadway Road out of the town is a pottery specialising in hand-thrown stoneware. Other local craft-workshops include sculpture, glass engraving and wood turning.

Close to Winchcombe is **Sudeley Castle**, a marvellous site, in private ownership. The castle has a long and distinguished history. It was so beautifully sited that Edward IV arrested Ralph Boteler, the owner, for treason, in order to acquire it for himself. As Boteler was taken away he turned to take his last look and said 'Sudeley Castle, thou art the traitor, not I'. The castle was of major importance at the end of the reign of Henry VIII. Henry came here with Katherine of Aragon and with Anne Boleyn; Thomas Seymour, brother of Jane, Henry's third wife, not only owned the castle but also married Katherine Parr, Henry's widow. Both Queen Mary and Queen Elizabeth spent time here as princesses and from here Lady Jane Grey, Thomas Seymour's niece, set out on the journey to London which was to end so tragically for her. Katherine Parr is buried in the castle church.

In addition to the castle itself, which has many art treasures, there are gardens and a pond with wild-fowl: in the parkland around the castle is an excellent children's playground, complete with a huge wooden fort.

PLACES OF INTEREST AROUND WINCHCOMBE

Sudeley Castle
Magnificent fortified building, partly ruined, set in beautiful parkland. Chapel with Katherine Parr's tomb. Good art collection in house. Frequent special exhibitions and excellent children's play area

Railway Museum, Winchcombe
Collection of BR memorabilia. Visitors receive a genuine old fashioned ticket!

Folk Museum, Winchcombe
Old Winchcombe Life

Belas Knap Long Barrow
Fine barrow with false portal

Hailes Abbey
Remains of abbey built in the thirteenth century. Part of cloisters still erect. Site museum contains the better relics

Notgrove Long Barrow
Good chambered barrow

Town Stocks, Winchcombe

Often during the summer there are special exhibitions in the castle or grounds, particularly at the Spring Holiday weekend when the site has a crafts exhibition which includes longbow making, archery demonstrations, and silversmithing.

There are several good walks from Winchcombe, but two of the best include visits to ancient sites. The first follows the Cotswold Way past the beautiful Wadfield Farm and Humblebee Cottages to the Belas Knap

V
4½m
1¾h
ooo
*

Sudeley Castle

long barrow, returning down the country lane towards the A46, but following the river back to the town before it is reached. The Belas Knap long barrow is one of the best preserved of the many such Stone Age burial chambers that can be seen in the Cotswolds. Much of its dry stone walling is original — a local craft that has remained unchanged for some 4,000 years. The apparent doorway of the barrow is, in fact, false: it was built either to fool grave robbers or, perhaps, to confuse evil spirits.

V
4½m
1½h
oo
**

The other walk visits Spoonley Roman Villa. This walk actually goes through Sudeley Park and then by path and track to the woods that now surround the villa. A circular route can be taken from here, but it is better to return by the same walk. The villa site has not been extensively excavated, but rooms and the courtyard can be discerned. The site has the feel of a ghostly ruin.

High on the wolds above Winchcombe is the source of the Windrush, and (at Cutsdean) of the Cotswolds name itself. In wet weather the stream has come a short distance by the time it reaches Cutsdean, but in dry weather it is barely a trickle until Ford, about a half mile further down the valley. It is only slight even there but it will become the most truly Cotswold of all the rivers whose valleys split the high wolds. It was high in this valley that an Anglo-Saxon called Cod had a farm on the wolds.

The walk along the footpath that follows the Windrush back towards its source from Cutsdean to Taddington, returning by the lane through the original wolds, is a link with history. If the stream is barely visible, the walk can be made along it, further down the valley from Ford to Temple Guiting, again returning along a high wold lane. **Temple Guiting** is a beautiful village, set among trees at the side of the stream. The stream has given it the second word in its name, derived from the same root as 'gushing'. Temple recalls the twelfth-century ownership of the manor by the Knights Templar. From here to **Guiting Power** the Windrush is not followed by footpaths, although the lane that connects the Guitings is delightful. Guiting Power is set on a tributary of the Windrush and is a straggling village, less picturesque than its more romantically named neighbour.

W
2m
¾h
oo
**

4 The Eastern Wolds_____

In the eastern Cotswolds the streams that drain down from the high Wolds are becoming rivers as they cross towards the Oxford Vale and the Thames. But the country is still Cotswold, even if the first village, or small town, that we visit — **Bourton-on-the-Water** — is slightly out of Cotswold character as an obvious tourist centre.

The commercial nature of Bourton should not prejudice the traveller to its great merits, and even some of the tourist traps are, in themselves, of considerable interest.

In best Cotswold tradition, the village is grouped around a river, the Windrush, already described as the typical Cotswold river. In its journey to the

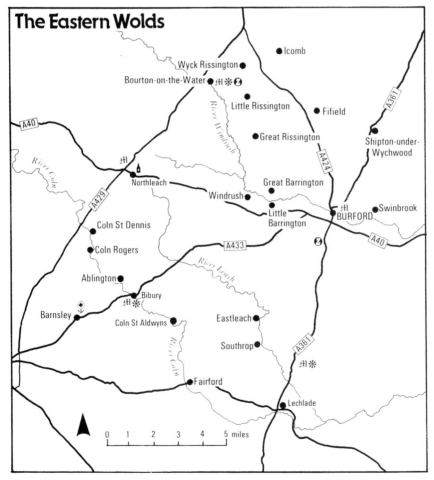

The Eastern Wolds

Icomb

Wyck Rissington

Bourton-on-the-Water

Little Rissington

Fifield

A361

A40

River Windrush

Great Rissington

Shipton-under-Wychwood

A424

Northleach

Windrush

Great Barrington

River Coln

A429

Little Barrington

BURFORD

Swinbrook

A40

Coln St Dennis

A433

Coln Rogers

River Leach

Ablington

Bibury

Barnsley

Coln St Aldwyns

Eastleach

Southrop

A361

Fairford

River Coln

Lechlade

0 1 2 3 4 5 miles

51

Bourton-on-the-Water

Thames Valley the Windrush is here wide and shallow, and is well set off by broad grassy banks. There are a number of bridges across it in the village, many of them only footpaths. Undoubtedly there have been bridges here for many years; indeed Bourton bridge that carries the A429 was once a Roman bridge supporting the Foss Way. Since bridges do not easily survive periods of neglect or age, the oldest now is around 230 years old. The village itself is much older; an Iron Age hillfort has been excavated at Salmonsbury, a little to the east. The original Norman church on Saxon foundations was largely demolished in 1784 and rebuilt with a dome, a unique feature in the Cotswolds. The Manor House in High Street was built in the twelfth century, rebuilt in the sixteenth century, re-built again in the late nineteenth and 'restored' in the early twentieth. The dovecote is noteworthy, and is believed to be of the sixteenth century. An even

better example of a dovecote can be seen in Sherborne Street where one house has the nest holes in its walls. Visitors to Bourton should not hurry, but those who can take only a short walk around it, seeing the church, houses and two of the bridges, will be well rewarded.

In Bourton High Street, behind the quaintly named Old New Inn, is the model village. The village modelled is Bourton itself, and so, of course, the model includes a model of the model! It is constructed on a 1:9 scale and is actually made in Cotswold stone. Also in High Street is the Butterfly Exhibition — a vibrant exhibition of live butterflies in glass-fronted tropical cases. The collection has recently been extended to include other exotic insects and spiders such as tarantulas, praying mantis and chameleons. Birdland is several acres of park, with hundreds of different species of birds, the majority of which are free-flying. In addition to the birds there is a tropical house and a shell exhibition.

T
1m
oo
*

*Village Life Exhibition,
Bourton-on-the-Water*

*The church and rectory,
Bourton-on-the-Water*

The park has good flower borders and a small art gallery devoted to paintings of wildlife.

For the more mechanically minded, the Motor Museum is housed in an old barley mill in the centre of the village. Here there are not only cars, but motorcycles and bicycles, as well as a good range of original die-cast models. Also in the High Street is the model railway where several hundred square feet of superb, detailed layout support a collection of British and overseas trains. Youngsters are even allowed to try their hands as drivers. Visitors to The Cotswold Perfumery are allowed free access to perfumes and other trial products and can watch the manufacturing processes, including the perfume blending laboratory. Most of the products are made on the site, but some processes are carried out only in the quiet months of winter.

To the east of Bourton are the Rissingtons of which (unusually in the Cotswolds) there are three rather than two. The best way to reach the first, Wyck Rissington, and indeed to see all

Folly Farm Waterfowl
Rare poultry and waterfowl
breeds

Motor Museum,
Collection of some thirty cars and
motor cycles, and a large collection
of old advertising signs. Housed in
eighteenth century mill

Birdland
Penguin rookery and free-flying
birds. Also exhibitions of shells and
wildlife artwork

Butterfly Exhibition
Butterflies in tropical flight cases.
Also tarantulas, stick insects,
praying mantis and chameleons

Model Railway
Excellent large layout with good
background and rolling stock

Model Village
Model of Bourton itself, including
a model of the model, all at 1/9th
scale

The Perfumery
Visits to the perfume blending
laboratory can be arranged

Village Life Exhibition
Edwardian village shop, forge, old
mill etc.

there a trackway leads to Little
Rissington, and a pathway beside its
church leads back to Bourton,
meandering between the ponds created
by the filling of gravel pits, after passing
Rissington Mill, inscribed 'Richard
Lane, Carpenter 1754'. An alternative
route is to follow the minor road back to
Bourton.

Wyck Rissington is the smallest of the
villages. The church is a massively-
constructed building where Gustav
Holst was once organist. The 17-year-
old Holst had his first professional
engagement on its hand-pumped organ:
he lived in the last cottage on the left of
the lane from the village towards the
Foss Way. The churchyard is as
interesting as the church. It has a living
cross trimmed from a yew tree 9ft high,
and a headstone on the grave of a gipsy,
marked 'of no fixed abode'. It is most
unusual to find a maze (beside the
church) in this small village: its origin is
equally remarkable. After World War II
the local vicar had a dream in which he
saw large numbers of people following
paths in a maze: an unseen figure
explained how the maze was to be
constructed. For several years, the vicar
laboured to construct the six hundred
yards of path and to plant the hedges of
willows, and it was opened on
Coronation Day 1953, although it is not
currently open to the public. At the
centre of the maze is a superb
Wellingtonia Pine. The maze has always
been regarded as a spiritual pilgrimage,
the pathway with its wrong turns being
seen as the path of life and the centre as
heaven. (Wolsey's Hampton Court maze
was constructed with a similar purpose.)
To the east of the village is Wyck
Beacon, whose summit is marked by a
triangulation pillar beside the road.

The next village, **Little Rissington**, lies
in the shadow of a large, but now almost
disused, RAF airfield. From Little
Rissington the walk can be extended, or
another started. This follows the
obvious trackway across to Great
Rissington, returning to Bourton by

three villages, is a circular tour from
Bourton. The walk leaves Bourton near
the Salmonsbury Camp, scene of an
important battle between rival Saxon
kingdoms over 1,350 years ago, and goes
across fields to Wyck Rissington. From

V
4½m
1½h
ooo
**

V
4½m
1½h
o
*

54

taking the minor road to Clapton-on-the-Hill over New Bridge and the distinct track to the right, towards woodland, some 300yd beyond.

Great Rissington is the most southerly and largest of the three villages. As with the northern pair it is a typical Cotswold village, though perhaps the only one whose main street rises 200ft so sharply. It overlooks the broad water meadows of the Windrush. The church still contains traces of a fourteenth-century wall painting.

On the opposite side of the broad Windrush valley from the Rissingtons is **Clapton-on-the-Hill**, another village whose name is almost as big as itself. Everything about Clapton appears tiny. The church is one of the smallest of all Cotswold churches, and the tiny collection of cottages surrounds a delightful gabled manor house. On a pleasant day the walk from Bourton to Clapton, reversing the final section of that above to reach the village, is a fine way of seeing the Windrush valley at close quarters, and from a high vantage point. The return to Bourton is either across fields, or by way of the local triangulation point, and the return is through delightful country lanes.

W
/₂m
2h
o

To the east of the Rissingtons is the A424 Stow-Burford road, and east again is the most easterly strip of the AONB, bordered on its Oxfordshire side by a railway line. In this eastern strip is a collection of small villages leading down through largely uninhabited high wold to Wychwood, Icomb, Westcote, Idbury and Fifield, each in its way delightful. Icomb Place is an imposing house, chiefly fifteenth century, though much restored and not open to the public. About ³/₄ mile west of the village is Guy's Folly, a pair of towers, one of the Cotswold examples of this particularly British eccentricity. At **Fifield** is the Merrymouth Inn, a good name even if it does derive from the name of the Norman Lord de Muremouth, and not (directly) from the landlord.

Below these villages, on the eastern side, is the Evenlode valley. Near the river, at Bruern, stood an early Cistercian Abbey, though nothing of it now remains. There is a delightful walk through the parkland where the abbey once stood, past the original fish pond, out through woods and across fields to Shipton-under-Wychwood. The return, by lanes bordering Bruern Wood, is equally attractive.

As mentioned above, the eastern boundary of the AONB is the railway line, but as this almost exactly follows the Evenlode, the river valley can be regarded as a more natural boundary. On the river towards Stow is Bledington, an attractive old village that clusters around a green and a stream, strictly only a tributary of the Evenlode itself.

Further down the Evenlode valley are those villages which lie 'under Wychwood'. This phrase, added to the names of the villages Milton, Shipton and Ascott, refers to the position of the villages beneath the Wychwood Forest, which once extended over a large area around Burford and even towards Bourton. It was famous as a deer forest and the inhabitants of Burford enjoyed the right to hunt there on one day each year. This privilege, together with poaching which was limited to the other 364 days, produced a saying that 'a Burford labourer ate as much venison in a week as a London Alderman in a year'. The forest is now much depleted. Indeed no part of it now lies within the Cotswold area, although the last surviving large area, a National Nature Reserve, is only two miles east of Shipton-under-Wychwood.

Shipton-under-Wychwood had a considerable reputation in the eighteenth and nineteenth centuries for lawlessness, presumably arising from the poaching in Wychwood Forest. It had inns that were clearly poaching inns, and the poachers and petty criminals seem to have carried on with little fear of detection. One stranger who called at an inn in the late nineteenth century opened his purse too readily and was buried in

V
5m
2h
oo

an unnamed grave in the churchyard. The poachers were not always successful. One man brought news of a remarkably fine deer that browsed each night at the edge of the forest. A gang went out that evening and shot the animal, a gipsy's donkey; but such was the honour among thieves that the men were forced to buy another.

Shipton Court, at the southern end of the town, is a lovely building, surrounded by fine yew trees, said to be haunted by the ghost of Sir John Reade. Sir John was a drunkard who owned the house in the mid-nineteenth century. His drinking partner was his butler and one night after a particularly heavy session the butler attempted to ring for yet more bottles. Sir John, sufficiently drunk, threw the bell rope over a picture to stop him, but the butler climbed up to retrieve it. He slipped (or was pushed) and fell into the fireplace, where he was impaled on a fire dog. Shipton was alive with the story of murder, but accidental death was recorded. Whatever the truth, Sir John never went drinking again and he died a deeply troubled man in 1868. His ghost was often seen afterwards and even an exorcism has not, apparently, stopped the haunting. A happier, and no less attractive building is the quaintly named Shaven Crown Inn which looks remarkably similar to Prior's Manse in Broadway.

Further south, **Swinbrook**, like the majority of local villages, also has a wealth of poaching stories. In the most famous, two Swinbrook men were out one night when they discovered a well-liked keeper who had been shot. The two men carried him back to the Hit and Miss Inn in Swinbrook — the name itself indicating poaching. The keeper, John Millins, died, and the two men were tried for murder, found guilty and hanged. Some years later a man dying in nearby Leafield confessed that he, not the Swinbrook men, had killed Millins accidentally, thinking he was a deer. The tree under which the keeper was found is still known as Millins' Oak. In

Swinbrook Church is the Fittiplace monument, a pair of wall tombs where six men of the family are stacked in threes, one on top of the other, each lying on his right side and looking at the visitor.

From here it is only a short drive to the beautiful ruin of Minster Lovell Hall, constructed around 1430 by Lord Lovell. It is close to the Windrush, and although there is little to see — some of the Great Hall and a tower — the ruin is overwhelmingly romantic. The small village church is dedicated to St Kenelm, whose tomb may be seen in Winchcombe.

Nearby **Fulbrook** was the home of Tom, Dick and Harry, perhaps the first of all such trios. In this case they were the Dunsdons, sons of a respectable family, who turned to theft, at first on a small scale. Emboldened by success they turned highwaymen, robbing the Oxford to Gloucester coach, a crime which made them famous and much sought after. Their nightly haunt was an inn with another poaching name, The Bird in the Hand, at Capp's Lodge. Though the inn has long gone, the name survives at Capp's Lodge Farm, a mile out of Fulbrook to the right on the Shipton road. One night at the inn, where they seem to have been safe from capture, they drank too much and boasted of their scheme to rob the local manor of Tangley Hall. Their plan was passed to the householder who called in the constables. A shutter for looking at visitors normally guarded a hole in the front door of the manor, but that night the shutter was removed; an arm, put through the hole to feel for the door key, was lassoed by the constables and tied to the doorhandle. Outside, there was much swearing, followed by a shout of 'Cut it' and the arm fell through the hole on to the floor. The door was opened but the brothers had escaped. Dick was never seen again, and it was assumed that he had bled to death following the amputation. The brothers continued in crime until they over-reached themselves one day by quarrelling with the landlord of the Bird in the Hand. They were promptly arrested, taken to Gloucester for trial, found guilty and sentenced to death. Tom, hurt during their arrest, limped to the scaffold. Harry kept encouraging him, telling him that it made small difference that he had only one leg since he had only a little time to stand. After execution the bodies were brought back and gibbetted, probably on the Gibbet Tree to the side of the Fulbrook-Shipton road a little north of Capp's Lodge. Such executions and gibbeting were very common at that time and not far from this tree is the sinisterly named Habber Gallows Hill, about three miles north of Burford on the A424 to Stow.

An interesting part in the story of the Dunsdon brothers was played by the village of Icomb. They had a cottage there which was connected by an underground passage to the nearby wood where their horses were stabled and the loot was hidden.

From Fulbrook it is only a short journey to **Burford**, an elegant town with a wide, steep, main street leading down to the river Windrush from the Wolds. For a town that is now so solid a part of the landscape it is remarkably young, for when the Romans wanted to cross the Windrush they brought Akeman Street down river to Asthall, shunning, perhaps, the north-facing slope at Burford. By early Saxon times there was a settlement here, grouped around the fort of the same name, and by AD 752 the ford had become important, on the route from Wessex to Mercia. In that year the two kingdoms fought here at Burford. (As a link with history a midsummer festival was recently held here at which the dragon and giant, the standards of the two Saxon armies, were carried in procession.) Almost a thousand years later, in 1649, following the Civil War, Burford was again the scene of bloodshed. At nearby Salisbury, some of the Parliamentarian soldiers mutinied after losing faith in Cromwell,

who they believed had become a tyrant; they further feared being posted to Ireland. They marched to Burford where they were arrested with little gunfire and no bloodshed. The men were imprisoned in the church for three days while Cromwell decided what to do next. Finally a token group of three men was taken into the churchyard and shot. To ensure that the other mutineers were 'encouraged' by the executions, some were forced to watch. One of these was Anthony Sedley and in the church the visitor can still see, scratched on the rim of the font: 'Anthony Sedley Prisner 1649'. The visitor may also notice the monument to Lord Chief Justice Tanfield, an imposing tomb, erected by his wife, with a Latin inscription bemoaning the burial in such a backwater of so important a man as her husband.

There is only one way to see Burford — on foot. It has a quite remarkable collection of fourteenth- to sixteenth-century houses. The almshouses in Church Lane date from the mid-fifteenth century while the cottages in High Street near the bridge are 100 years older. High Street itself has many notable buildings. The Corner House is sixteenth century, slightly older than the delightfully named Rampant Cat. Hill House, on the western side, is mainly fourteenth century. The Tolsey, or Court House (now housing a museum), is a sixteenth-century house with elegant bay windows. Here can be seen the charters of the original town, dating from the thirteenth century, together with seals, which may be as old, and the sixteenth-century town mace.

South of Burford on the A361 is the Cotswold Wildlife Park. Here a variety of animals, both large and small, are kept in expansive enclosures. There are special houses for reptiles and tropical birds. In addition, there are landscaped gardens, a narrow gauge railway, adventure playground and pets' corner.

From Burford, the traveller following the Windrush back towards the wolds

T
1½m
ooo
*

57

Places of Interest Around Bibury and Burford

Arlington Mill Museum, Bibury
Mill complete with working waterwheel. Collection of agricultural implements, and arts and crafts. William Morris room

Cotswold Countryside Collection, Northleach
New museum based on the Lloyd-Baker collection of agricultural implements and wagons, housed in Northleach prison, whose history is displayed in the old cell block

Arlington Row, Bibury
Fine row of early seventeenth-century weavers' cottages

Trout Farm, Bibury
Modern farm for restocking and eating. Fish on sale

Cotswold Woollen Weavers, Filkins
Craftsman-woven cloth

Cotswold Wildlife Park, Nr Burford
Large site with white rhinos, tigers, zebra etc, but also tapirs and red pandas. Also smaller mammals, birds and insect house

Minster Lovell Hall
Romantic remains of fifteenth-century hall

Tolsey Museum, Burford
Collection of seals and charters for the town, dating from the thirteenth century

Swinford Museum, Filkins
Collection of farming and country craft tools

Barnsley House Gardens
House not open. Garden includes fine collection of rare shrubs and trees, Gothic summerhouse and good tree avenues

Cross Tree Gallery, Filkins
Displays work of contemporary Cotswold artists

V
8m
3h
oooo
*

should not use the A40, quick though it is, but the minor road that leaves the A424 over the Burford Bridge. There is a superb walk along the country lanes that link Burford to the Barringtons on each side of the Windrush: it starts just over the Windrush Bridge at the bottom of High Street. The walker in the meadow on the northern side of the river stands amongst grasses, reeds and farm animals, while across the water, the town starts instantly, a whole collection of interesting town houses being just a stone's throw away. On the return journey the walker passes the fifteenth-century Lamb Inn and the Priory, which still houses a monastic order.

The walk first goes through **Taynton**, famous for the quality of the building stone that came from its quarries. Blenheim Palace and some Oxford Colleges are of Taynton stone. The village itself is a tapestry in stone, set at such an angle of the Windrush Valley that it may be seen almost in complete detail as the traveller aproaches. Above Taynton, the Windrush has crossed from Gloucestershire into Oxfordshire and a mile beyond the border are the Barringtons, Great and Little.

Barrington stone was not much sought after as a primary building stone, but it was once used to repair Westminster Abbey, being floated down the Windrush and the Thames to London. If the stone was less sought

Monument in Great Barrington church

after, however, its masons were not. The most famous, Thomas Strong, considered by Wren to be the finest in England, was a leading mason contractor on St Paul's Cathedral. He actually laid the foundation stone himself, though he died before the cathedral was completed. He left money in his will 'to make a way between the Barrington Bridges that two men may go a front to carry a corpse in safety'. The road, still known as Strong's Causeway, is included in the walk described above. After Thomas's death his brother Edward took over as Master Mason of England, and laid the final stone of St Paul's.

Great Barrington Church is famous for its marble monument to two children of the Bray family who died of smallpox

in 1720. The monument, a sculpted marble mural, amongst the finest in England, was long thought to be the work of Francis Bird, Sir Christopher Wren's favourite sculptor, but experts now believe that it is actually by Christopher Cass. There is also a notable memorial to Captain Edmund Bray, clad in Tudor armour but wearing his sword on his right side, not his left. He murdered a man in anger but was pardoned by Elizabeth I, after swearing never again to draw his sword with his right hand. Barrington Park was, and is, a walled deer park in which Earl Talbot built his fine mansion after the style of Palladio. The mansion sits on a natural terrace, but as this was too far from the river for a good view, the river was moved slightly!

Northleach Church

To reach **Little Barrington**, Strong's Causeway is crossed between the two arms of the Windrush. The land between the two teems with plant and animal life. Little Barrington itself is spread out along the southern Windrush bank to such an extent that it seems larger than its 'greater' neighbour.

Upstream of the Barringtons is **Windrush**, a tiny village, far smaller than its name leads the visitor to expect. A picture book village, almost every building is a fine example of its type. Special note should be made of the seventeenth-century corn mill.

From Windrush village mill, a path crosses the water meadows near the river with its lilies and trout, and then follows the Sherborne brook back to Sherborne village. To return, the lane back to Windrush is a delight, but the stronger walker can go ³/₄ mile north on the lane to Clapton and take the distinct track eastward that crosses the Windrush.

From the far side another track goes southward to a lane leading back to the Barringtons.

Sherborne village is strangely positioned, strung out along the stream, but distinctly divided by Sherborne Park, another large manor house. This originally belonged to Winchcombe Abbey and was used by the abbot when he came to check the sheep shearing; the Sherborne Valley has always been good farming land. Continue along the Sherborne Brook valley for another 3 miles, to **Farmington**, the last village on the minor road from Burford to Northleach. The village is an ancient site, with a long barrow and some old fortifications to the west.

From Farmington it is a short journey to **Northleach**. This very special village, or small town, is best viewed from a distance particularly along the minor road from Farmington. Northleach is then seen in the valley below, as the

V
3m
1h
ooo
*
or
V
6m
2h

oo
**

60

Northleach

visitor drops off the Wold, in front of the unfortunate backdrop of electricity pylons and lines, but from this northern side the church stands up from behind the houses. In villages all over the Cotswolds the cottages are grouped around churches, most of which are not only at the heart of the village, but also at the heart of its interest and history. But where the wool merchants' money was used to finance complete buildings, so that the church is all of one architectural period and enriched by fine stonemasonry, the church is not only at the heart of the village but dominates it completely. It is generally agreed that the three finest wool churches in the Cotswolds are at Cirencester, Chipping Campden and at Northleach. Cirencester is a major town and absorbs the church's presence; Campden, though smaller, is a town nonetheless; but here at Northleach the church does truly dominate. It was constructed in the

fifteenth century on the site of a previous church, though of that very little indeed survives; as notable for its exterior work as for its interior, it is the interior that holds the attention, for there is a unique collection of memorial brasses, the finest in Britain, almost exclusively of the wool merchants who raised the church. Most of the figures on the brasses have the traditional wool pack at their feet and some have sheep as well. The brass of John Fortey who died in 1459 is the largest (5ft), and it dates from the best period of brass engraving. Within the church a leaflet details the brasses, giving their ages, and translating the Latin inscriptions. The inscriptions include a mix of Latin and Arabic numerals, and the arms of the English City of Calais. Few of the buildings in the rest of the village can compare with the church, but its position, on the main A40, means that there is much traffic noise.

There are other buildings of interest in Northleach. A little to the west of the village, at the cross-roads between the A40 and A429, is the old village police station and prison, built in 1790 by Sir Onesiphorus Paul, a gentleman who had not only an extraordinary Christian name, but also an interest in penal reform and the welfare of prisoners. At a time when a miscreant could expect his sentence to include not only imprisonment but a straw bed, no water or sanitation, no exercise and typhus, Sir Onesiphorus built this prison with exercise yards, separate rooms for sleeping, baths and a sick bay. It was not just a prison, but also a 'house of correction'. It is now a museum. There is a history of the prison in the cell block, and the Cotswold Countryside Collection, a history of agriculture in the Cotswolds area built mainly around the Lloyd-Baker collection of implements and wagons.

To the south of the A40 from Northleach to Burford, the Cotswolds are split by fertile river valleys, along which the villages have grown. The wolds of this southern section are perhaps more sparsely populated than in the north. Certainly the difference between populated valley and empty wold is very striking. The first valley was cut deep by the river Leach that flows by Northleach itself; indeed it springs close to the village. In its upper reaches the Leach drains bleak wold, but it does not have the character of the Windrush. Neither does it have, except in its lower reaches, the prettiness of the Coln. Nevertheless it is a fine valley, and gives its name to Lechlade, the town that actually separates the Cotswolds from the Thames valley. Remarkably it eluded the Ordnance Survey map makers: OS Sheet 163 (Landranger Series) has the river disappearing at Kilkenny Farm, south of Northleach, only to reappear a little north of the Eastleaches, five miles away! Those who want to be convinced of the river's continuity should follow it in this section where it crosses Akeman Street.

Short, enjoyable walks on the wolds around Akeman Street can be linked with some country lanes to make a complete route from Northleach to Eastleach which is never far away from the river. It is best to go by way of the villages, the essence of the Cotswolds. First is **Eastington**, one of two Gloucestershire villages of the same name. This is the prettier, a hamlet on the banks of the stream. A mile or so on from the village is Lodge Park, another deer park, which has a very fine long barrow. The Lodge was built around 1630 by John Dutton, a friend of Cromwell, who was allowed to stock it with deer from Wychwood Forest. The building was only used to watch coursing in the park. The coursing was by greyhounds, as usual, but the quarry was deer, not hares. This cruel practice was regarded as good sport by the rich gentry; one needed to be rich, because Dutton allowed anyone to try his dogs at a price of half-a-crown for each dog, together with ten old pence for the 'slipper' who released the deer.

Aldsworth is accepted as a Leach valley village, even though by now the river is a mile away. It is really a high wold village, and an attractive one with a fine set of gargoyles on the church.

The prettier end of the Leach valley is reached at **Eastleach**. This is divided by the river into two villages each having its own church. Eastleach Turville is the larger, the second half of the name derived from that of an early Norman lord. Eastleach Martin is named from its church, although this part of the village is known locally as Bouthrop. The whole village was granted to Gloucester Abbey in the thirteenth century by the lord of the manor, who set the yearly rent at one pound of wax! An interesting sidelight on the power of the church in such villages only 250 years ago is shown by A. P. Ledger's work on the Eastleach parish records. These show that in 1747 a small group of village folk was 'presented' by the vicar to the Bishop of

Keble Bridge, Eastleach

Gloucester at Cirencester. One was accused of not having been to church for at least three months. The parish clerk was presented 'for defamation and scandal in saying that I had wronged him!' But worst of all, Anne Cock was presented 'as lying under a common fame of fornication, which I verily believe to be upon just grounds, she being in all appearances big with child'!

In Eastleach one must visit Keble's Bridge, the most photographed part of the village, perhaps also of the Cotswolds. The most famous of the Kebles whose name is commemorated here is John Keble, the poet and leader of the Oxford Movement in the early nineteenth century. Keble was rector of both Eastleach churches, and of Southrop, for eight years. The footpath-only bridge, made of large, flat stone slabs on low supports, is little different from the clapper bridge of prehistory.

The walk from Northleach enters Eastleach by crossing Macaroni Downs, probably named from the late eighteenth century London Macaroni Club. The Macaronis were young rich playboys who frequented the nearby Bibury racecourse. They were famous for extravagant, Italian clothes and enormous wigs, though it is not known why the Downs and one or two local farms should be named after them.

The best walk in the Leach valley is not that described above, but from Eastleach down to Southrop. It follows paths beside the river and returns along a path and lane, crossing the river at each of the villages. At **Southrop** the Leach is a beautiful sight, as wide as a road and only a hand's breadth deep. The village itself is as attractive as Eastleach, though less well-known, perhaps because it lacks a photogenic footbridge. But it does have a fine sixteenth-century manor house, a very old and tiny church, an array of excellent stone cottages, and a carefully restored seventeenth-century corn mill. To the west of the Leach, just the other side of the A361, is the village of **Filkins**, where the Swinford Museum specialises in agricultural and rural domestic exhibits.

V
2m
1h
ooo
*

63

Arlington Row, Bibury

The other river valley in the area south of Northleach is the Coln. It runs under another Foss Bridge on the A429 Cirencester to Stow road, and then flows through a succession of delightful villages before flowing through Fairford to join the Thames near Lechlade. For almost its entire way it can be followed on foot by path and country lane. It is a long but worthwhile walk which will be given in sections.

From Foss Bridge to Quenington the river can be followed on either side. This sectioned walk gives single way distances between villages:

V
8m
2¾h
ooo
*

Foss Bridge to Coln St Dennis	½ mile
Coln St Dennis to Coln Rogers	1 mile
Coln Rogers to Ablington	2 miles
Ablington to Bibury	1 mile
Bibury to Coln St Aldwyns	2½ miles
Coln St Aldwyns to Quenington	1 mile

From Foss Bridge the first village is the tiny **Coln St Dennis**, with a Norman church on the banks of the river. Its tower has a strange opening couplet to an inscription on its inner, northern, wall. It reads 'Heare lyes my body fast inclosed within this watery ground; by my precious soule it cannot nowe be founde': the memorial is to Joan Burton who died in 1631. Beyond Coln St Dennis is the tiny hamlet of Calcot, a typical Cotswold valley hamlet, with pretty stone cottages and river.

Coln Rogers has an even older, Saxon, church. The name derives from Roger de Gloucester, the lord of the manor in the mid-twelfth century. The village was then known as Coln on the Hill, but this was changed by the grateful Abbot of Gloucester when Sir Roger granted him the manor.

Winson has a fine manor house and a long stretch of river before the next village, **Ablington**, which has not one, but two, large houses — the Manor from the late sixteenth and the House about 100 years later. The House is

64

Lower Slaughter

Fosseway House, Stow-on-the-Wold

Village Life Exhibition, Bourton-on-the-Water

Frocester Hill

The Swan Hotel, Bibury

distinguished by its stone lions which came from the Houses of Parliament.

Bibury, the largest and most famous of the Coln valley villages, is split by the main A433. Here, too, is a Saxon church, a truly great one. Some of the Saxon work was so fine that the originals were taken to the British Museum, and one sees casts on show here. Part of the churchyard is known as the Bisley Piece. William Morris, the Pre-Raphaelite artist, also connected with Broadway, described the village as the most beautiful in England. It is easy to understand his judgement when one walks along the road beside the Coln. On one side are the cottages of Arlington Row, across a clear stream in which large trout swim, and on the other the more substantial houses and the Swan Hotel, dating from the late 1700s

and among the best restaurants in the area. Modern Bibury is actually an amalgam of several pieces and the visitor will find much of interest. Bibury hamlet is grouped around the church, but there is a second hamlet at Arlington, on the hill behind Arlington Row. Further downstream, where the walker has to leave the Coln for a short time, is Bibury Court, a well-proportioned mansion of the early seventeenth century, superbly sited near the river, with a fine backdrop of trees. At the road bridge over the Coln is Arlington Mill, a seventeenth-century building on a site mentioned in the Domesday Book. It was both a cloth mill and a corn mill, but now houses a museum of country crafts, including a working water mill. There is also a collection of William Morris memorabilia, perhaps in deference to his

Coln St Aldwyns

opinion of the village. At the side of the mill is the Bibury trout farm which breeds for release as well as for eating. The various stages of fish development can be followed, and the trout can be seen underwater in a floodlit mill race.

Arlington Row is best reached by crossing an ancient footbridge. The cottages are now owned by the National Trust, but were originally weavers' cottages, built for the outside work force which supplied cloth for fulling at Arlington Mill.

The final villages of the Coln before it heads for Fairford and the Thames are **Coln St Aldwyns** and **Quenington**. The former has a green dominated by a magnificent horse chestnut tree, and is as good as any of the more northerly villages. It is separated from Quenington

by part of Williamstrip Park; the house here was built by a Speaker of the House of Commons.

Between Coln and Cirencester is another stretch of high wold. Barnsley Wold is named from the village **Barnsley** on the A433 Cirencester to Bibury road. The village is set on the Welsh Way, an old track over the Wolds used by the Welsh cattle drovers. The number of such drove roads through the area explains the number of inns called 'Butcher's Arms', as the slaughtering of the cattle occurred at various points on the journey to London. The most famous attraction here is Barnsley House, set in an excellent garden with numerous rare shrubs. The gothic summerhouse and the temple in the garden have been brought here recently.

5 Roman Cotswolds

This section of the guide deals with the southern end of the northern Cotswolds, the strip of country between Gloucester and Cirencester sandwiched between the A40 and the A417. It is not, in fact, as arbitrary as it seems. It has been said that if you scratch Gloucestershire then you find Rome beneath, and this is the heart of Roman Gloucestershire and, therefore, Roman Cotswold. This is the land between *Corinium* and *Glevum*, including, at Chedworth, some of the

finest remains of any Roman villa in Britain.

Cirencester was the second largest town of Roman Britain, with an area of 240 acres (only London was bigger). It grew up around a fort built about AD50, about 100 years after Julius Cæsar had come, and gone. He did not get as far as Cirencester; his visit was a reconnaissance rather than an actual invasion. In AD43 there was a true invasion and the Roman names of some

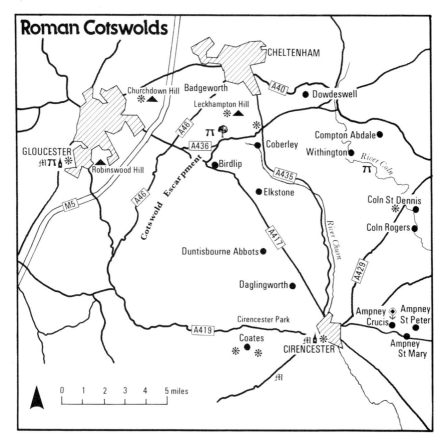

Cirencester

---

of their towns reflect the military nature of the campaign. *Caer Coryn* was the native name for the settlement where Cirencester is now, from *Caer* a 'fort', and *Coryn* the 'top part'. The latter is interesting because it probably refers to the Churn, the river that runs through Cirencester, being the highest source of the River Thames. As the frontier moved and the area became more peaceful, the town's name was changed to *Corinium*. The Saxons who followed the Romans changed it back to the original name. Since, however, the Saxons used *Ceastre* for *Caer* the town was then *Ceastre Coryn* which was reversed to become *Coryn Ceastre* or Cirencester.

The town was built at the intersection of three crucial roads — the Foss Way, Akeman Street and Ermin Street. For those wishing to know more of Roman *Corinium* there is no better place than the Museum in Park Street. There, besides the many finds that have been unearthed from beneath the present town during excavations, the visitor will find reconstructions of numerous aspects of Roman life including a mosaic-maker's workshop. Also on display, and indeed one of the most famous Roman relics in Britain, is an early link between the Romans and the Christian church, a world-famous word square painted on plaster and found in

New Road in the nineteenth century. The museum has many other fine exhibits, while the Roman amphitheatre is still visible on the south side of the bypass road that passes south of the town.

The town remained Roman, or rather Romano-British, until 577, when it was destroyed by the Saxons. The destruction was so total that when the Saxons built their own town on the site, the Roman square plan was not used. However, the town was soon important again; it was a royal city in Saxon times and was visited by King Canute; in Norman times a great abbey was built here. Nothing now remains of it, as it was completely destroyed at the dissolution. But the abbot was also rector of the parish church, and that building still survives.

As Cirencester is the largest of the truly Cotswold towns, it naturally has a fine church. The town was important in medieval times as a wool centre; the benefactions of the local merchants were extremely generous; the church is not only the largest in the Cotswolds but one of the largest in England: indeed it is larger than several British cathedrals. It is not in a formal encircling churchyard but amongst the other town buildings. Inside, the church is a rare treasure house, the plate being among the most interesting in England. The Boleyn Cup, a gilt cup made for Queen Anne Boleyn in 1535 and bearing her family crest, is the most famous, although a pair of jug-shaped flagons from 1570 is, perhaps, the finest. Although the memorial brasses are also worthy of notice, the chief interest lies in the matrimonial achievements of the wool merchants. William Prelatte had two wives, while Reginald Spycer had four. Robert Page had only one wife, but six sons and eight daughters. A much later brass shows Rebecca Powell with her two husbands.

Reginald Spycer, commemorated here, was instrumental in the arrest and execution, at the town, of the earls who led a rebellion against Henry IV. The action prevented a civil war and the grateful king gave the town a handsome reward with which the church tower was built. It is a fine work and can be climbed, one of the few in the area that is open. The climb, up a narrow and very tightly spiralled staircase, is hard work, but the view of the town, park and surrounding countryside is worthwhile.

No trip to Cirencester is complete without a tour of the town. The church is in the Market Place and a street market is still held there twice a week. South through the Market Place towards Dyer's Street, the Corn Hall, a fine Victorian building, is on the right: it is the site of the craftsmen's market, a twice-monthly market and exhibition of local crafts. All crafts are represented, and work can be bought or commissioned. In Dyer's Street the Bear Inn is a classic timber-framed house with overhangs. At the end on the right is Lewis Lane, and, on the right again, Cricklade Street. To the left here are the Cirencester Workshops, a collection of craft units housed in an old brewery. There is a gallery, shop and coffee house. Left again, in Cripps Road, is the Cirencester Brass Rubbing Centre where the visitor can produce his own rubbing, from resin replicas, of some of the best brasses in the country.

Cricklade Street leads back past the Market Place again and allows a left turn into Blackjack Street, reputedly named from a statue of St John on the church, whose stone became dark with age. Straight on from here is Cirencester Park. The Corinium Museum is on the right as one enters Park Street. On the right, in Thomas Street, is Weavers Hall or St Thomas' Hospital, an almshouse set up in the early fifteenth century for destitute weavers. Coxwell Street, running almost parallel to Thomas Street, is narrow and can hardly have changed over the centuries: on one side are the houses of the rich wool merchants, while on the other are those of the poor weavers.

At the end of Thomas Street, a left

T
1m
ooo
*

turn leads into Dollar Street (named from Dole Hall, the abbey almonry); this leads on to Gloucester Street where there is a further set of almshouses, known as St Lawrence's. Spital Gate Lane contains the town's third group of almshouses, St John's Hospital, originally founded by Henry II but rebuilt early last century. Spital Gate, named from this building and known locally as Saxon Arch, was actually a Norman gatehouse of the abbey — standing at the junction with Grove Lane. From the Arch the walker returns to Lewis Lane by following the River Churn across the Abbey grounds. To the west of the town is Cirencester Park, famous for its polo tournaments. The house itself was built in the early eighteenth century and is not open to the public. Externally, it is generally considered to be a failure; even Lord Bathurst, who commissioned it, apparently agreed. Thinking aloud to Alexander Pope, after seeing what he had received for his money, he wondered 'How comes it to look so oddly bad?'. The park itself is open to the public and there are several picnic sites and forestry and farm trails which can be followed. Polo is played on Sundays during the polo league season and the very quiet or lucky walker may see one of the fallow deer that still roam the park.

The park is, strictly, entered only from the town end. It is private, but the public is allowed in under certain conditions, but *no* dogs. To the north, Overley Woods, and to the west, at the end of Broad Ride, certain areas of the park can be reached directly, but it must be borne in mind that the parkland is private, and entrance depends upon the goodwill of the landowner. It offers fine walking, particularly along the Broad Ride to the Ten Rides meeting point. To the north-east is Alfred's Hall, a folly of Lord Bathurst, from about 1720. It is dated 1085 and was built complete with black oak and rusty armour. An early visitor is said to have commented on its antiquity to the caretaker, and received the astonishing reply 'Oh this is nothing, my lord intends building one 200 years older shortly!'

As the boundary of the AONB on this southern edge near Cirencester has been drawn along Akeman Street, certain villages have been removed from the Cotswolds. Although this guide attempts to maintain the strict boundary, straying only to visit an especially fine attraction, an exception must be the three villages close to the Ampney Brook, two miles east of Cirencester. These can be linked by a walk that starts from Ampney Crucis and goes south of the A417 by a path that crosses the Ampney Brook, and the

Chedworth Church

main road itself, to reach Ampney St Peter. An easy walk north from here leads to Ampney St Mary, from which pathways lead back to the start. The largest of the villages is the first, **Ampney Crucis**, not named from the remarkable and ancient cross in the churchyard, but from the church itself, dedicated to the Holy Cross. The church contains the remains of wall paintings at least 600 years old. The village also has an excellent mill, and the gardens of Ampney Park, a fine Jacobean manor, are open to visitors. There are beautiful trees and a lake with an interesting collection of water fowl. **Ampney St Mary** is away from the brook that gives the villages their name. It, too, is named from its church which contains a superb collection of wall paintings, some of which make the 600-year-old Crucis paintings appear young. Sadly, as with most such medieval wall paintings, the Puritans, who felt that such works were idolatrous, have mutilated much of the work. South of St Mary is **Ampney St**

Peter, which is on the Brook. The stone cottages of the village and the nearness of the stream are typically Cotswold.

The area between Cirencester and Cheltenham-Gloucester is dominated by the valleys of the rivers Churn and Coln. It is the latter that we first describe. A little way south of Foss Bridge where the A429 crosses the Coln is a trail on Denfurlong Farm, a dairy farm, the operation of which is explained to the visitor. The trail walker is allowed into the secrets of crop rotation and given a glimpse of the way modern farming can be used to assist wildlife conservation. Only a mile from the farm is **Chedworth** village, not on the Coln itself, but on a steep-sided tributary. The village is attractively placed on both sides of the steep valley. Those who find the village from Denfurlong do not get the full flavour of this side of the valley, which is better approached from Foss Bridge up the quaintly named Pancake Hill — certainly not as flat as a pancake. The village clings to the steep sides of the

valley, the cottages appearing to grow
out of it; indeed, they have more rows of
windows that open away from the hill
than open on to it. The village once had
a railway line, and the skill with which
the engineers laid its track, in view of the
steep and deep sides of the upper Coln
Valley and the limited gradients
necessary for locomotives, is
astonishing. The travellers on this line,
from Cheltenham to Cirencester, passed
through some excellent countryside,
even if the line did have considerable
lengths of embanked track. The idea of
creating a footpath along the disused
trackway has not been pursued with
great vigour: as it penetrates the heart of
Chedworth visitors could visit the
woods, while keeping away from some
of the nature reserves that the woods
now house.

The woods themselves stretch from
the outskirts of Chedworth village right
across to the Coln valley and the Roman

villa, and follow the valley itself from
Stowell Park, near the Foss Way — the
A429 — up to Withington. This is the
first section of wooded valley that so
characterises the Cotswolds in the area
around the Stroud valley. The wood is
true British deciduous forest,
intermingled with some conifer, and as
such is a delight. The roads that follow
the Coln Valley from Yanworth past the
Roman Villa towards Cassey Compton,
and then left through the wood, or from
Chedworth to Withington, are
delightful. On occasions they are
unfenced, the wood ending at the
roadside. The visitor can certainly sense
the past in the silence.

To reach Chedworth Roman Villa one
does *not* go the Chedworth village, as the
villa is in the Coln valley on a road going
west from Yanworth. A more suitable
way to approach the site is through the
woods from Chedworth village. There
are, in fact, several paths and bridleways

Yanworth Tithe Barn

from the village into the woods and on to the Villa. The walker can choose to go from the village or, perhaps better, take the minor road to Stowell, under the railway bridge and use the bridlepath that leaves this after it has risen steeply. This allows the benefit of excellent views of Chedworth itself.

The Roman Villa is often regarded as the finest in Britain. It is very large, with 32 rooms and separate bathrooms. Only when faced with the enormity of the building does the sophistication of the Romans strike home. The medieval period in Britain, with its hovels and superstitions, tends to obscure the fact that the Romans were a people of culture and builders of great skill. The villa remains have been covered to preserve them, and the best of the domestic articles that have been found are in a museum at the site. An interesting by-product of the Roman occupation is that the large European edible snail can be found at the site and in the nearby area.

Yanworth, mentioned as being on the route to the villa from the east, is a small hamlet set above the Coln, with fine barns near a church that includes an

Withington

ancient wall painting of a skeleton as Old Father Time. Further down river from Yanworth is Stowell and Stowell Park, where the mansion was constructed on the site of a house owned by the Tames, a rich woolstapler family from Northleach. The views from the outskirts of the park towards Chedworth woods and the river are breathtaking. The best are obtained by following the river to and from a well-sited pub, taking the path from Foss Bridge to Stowell Park and returning by path and lane on the opposite side of the river.

Withington is at the other end of the road from Yanworth that goes past Chedworth Villa. Its fine older part is set in the Coln Valley which is not too steep or deep at this point. The pleasant village has an inn, The Mill, recently constructed with stone from Northleach prison.

Above Withington the Coln is difficult to follow, not because the water is underground or insufficient, but because the head waters are not a single stream; one rises near Brockhampton, and another towards Dowdeswell. Which one is the Coln?

The western branch, towards Dowdeswell, flows past the pleasant hamlet of Foxcote, having sprung from below Foxcote Hill and the Kilkenny viewpoint, a nicely situated series of tiered car parks. The view is over the Gloucester Vale and the Severn, a wide vista not only towards the vale with the major towns of Gloucester, Cheltenham and Tewkesbury, but also of the distant Malverns.

Another head water flows to **Andoversford**, a small town that is mainly modern and suburban, and not really comparable with the villages of the lower valley. Beyond Andoversford is **Dowdeswell** where the reservoir is one of the few large expanses of water in the Cotswolds. The village looks out across this water, with the woods beyond, and from this distance has a fine view. To the south and east are two more parks. Sandywell Park, to the east, was described by Horace Walpole as

V
2½m
1h
oo
*

Compton Abdale

containing 'a square box of a house, very dirtily situated', but Upper Dowdeswell Manor, to the south, is a much nicer late sixteenth-century house. The name Dowdeswell is said to derive from a Saxon chief Dodo who also, with another called Odo, founded Tewkesbury.

Returning towards the Foss Way the village of **Compton Abdale** sits on the edge of high wold, above the Coln Valley. The village's beauty is enhanced by the small stream flowing down the main street. It is on the White Way, a very ancient trackway leading across the high wold. Before the advent of freezing, salt was used for preserving freshly-killed meat, and from earliest times tracks, known as Salt Ways or White Ways, were made across Britain to saltings. This particular way heads back across the wolds towards the Midlands, probably to the salt town of Droitwich.

W
4m
1½
½h
oo
*

The Way takes the traveller down to the Coln and up into Chedworth Woods. Beyond is open wold again. At the exit from the wood one is suddenly in the middle of a disused airfield. After being on a minor road in ancient woodland one is suddenly on a vast expanse of wide runway in altogether modern scenery. The White Way then crosses the high wolds of North Cerney Downs on a perfectly straight 4-mile section of trackway. Beyond the Down, the road drops down to Spital Gate in Cirencester, but we take the Churn, to follow it back towards Cheltenham.

Baunton is the first village, a neat hamlet whose church contains a lifesize fourteenth-century wall painting of St Christopher wading through a stream with fish. The whole painting is 4m by 3m and is the largest and best in the country.

W
7m
½h
oo
*

From Baunton, the river can be followed by a path on its eastern bank all the way to North Cerney, but the western bank is accompanied by the A435, good for motorists, but not for walkers. Instead, one should leave the road and go up the escarpment east of

---

PLACES OF INTEREST AROUND CHEDWORTH AND COBERLEY

Crickley Hill Country Park
Includes the remains of a hillfort that has been extensively excavated

Chedworth Roman villa
Perhaps the finest villa site in Britain. On-site museum contains the better relics from excavations

Denfurlong Farm Trail
Trail through working farm. Notice Boards on crops, animals etc.

Devil's Chimney, Leckhampton
Rock pinnacle. The remains of quarrying on the hill.

Seven Springs
Source of Churn or Thames

North Cerney to the Downs and follow the fine lane that was White Way, back towards Baunton.

Bagendon, a pleasant hamlet, is set a little way back from the river. It gives little indication now of the importance it once had in the Iron Age, for excavations suggest that the village is on the site of the massive, and well-fortified, capital of the Dobunni tribe.

Next up-river is **North Cerney**, famous for its exquisite church. It is not of one period, but has been lately renovated completely, in keeping with its original work. Outside it has lovely carved corbels, and on the south wall, a manticore can be found, with the body of a lion, red hair, the face and ears of a man, three rows of teeth and a tail complete with scorpion's sting. The beast also had a fine singing voice. For food it was said 'it myght fede on they Braynes'. Inside the notable fifteenth-

75

century nave roof has supports which rest on carved corbels.

Rendcomb is the next village from North Cerney, a pretty collection of riverside cottages with another park, constructed for another member of the Northleach Tame family. Between Rendcomb and Colesbourne there is no public river footpath, but there is one between Colesbourne (which also has a park, containing a good collection of rare shrubs) and Cowley, whose manor has a water garden fed from artificial lakes, themselves fed from the Churn. Above Colesbourne is the tiny village of Elkstone noted for the curious parish records of the Rev Prior, vicar from 1682 to 1725. He notes in 1704 that he 'buried the stinking residue of William Gwylliams', and in 1724 that he married Joseph Still and Mary Pool — 'For future reference: he gave me what he gave to the sexton: a single miserable shilling'.

Further up the Churn valley, as the water in the stream bed becomes shallower, is **Coberley**, where Sir Richard Whittington once lived at the hall (no longer extant). Sir Richard, the Dick of pantomime fame, was Lord Mayor of London on three occasions. His mother, Joan, married Sir William Whittington, after being widowed by Sir Thomas Berkley, the local squire. Sir Thomas survived the battle of Crecy and died about 1350. The church has a fine collection of monuments; the oldest, dating from 1295, is of Sir Giles de Berkley, an ancestor of Sir Thomas. The tomb, is, in fact, above a heart burial, the effigy knight clutching a heart. Such burials were common at the time, the heart being interred separately from the rest of the body. In this case the body of Sir Giles is at Little Malvern. The grass mound in the churchyard is where Sir Giles' favourite horse, Lombard, is buried. Animal burials in consecrated ground are unusual — Sir Giles must have been very influential.

The Churn springs at **Seven Springs**. They are at the side of the A436 and can be reached by descending to a small copse below road level. The tablet claims, in Latin, that this is the source of the Thames. Nowadays it is generally acknowledged that the Thames rises at Thameshead, a little way south-west of Cirencester. The claim of the Churn to be the true source is strong, however, in that it rises about 10 miles further from Lechlade than the more southerly headwater.

An excellent walk from here is to follow the Cotswold Way to the Devil's Chimney on Leckhampton Hill. It follows the escarpment slope around Charlton Kings Common and Leckhampton Hill. The view of Cheltenham in the valley below, and of the edge, is very good. The Devil's Chimney itself is a rock pinnacle, a remnant of quarrying on the hill.

Leckhampton itself had an interesting group of manorial lords. One, Gilbert de Clare, was killed at Bannockburn when he was just 23 and is buried at Tewkesbury. Another family, the Giffards, from nearby Brimpsfield, built the original court. One of the lord's four sons founded Worcester College, Oxford, two were prominent local gentry, and the fourth was hanged for robbing the King's baggage train near Birdlip.

To the south is the Crickley Hill Country Park, built around the most completely excavated hillfort on the Cotswolds. In the summer months visitors can frequently watch excavations in progress, and receive a guided tour. At other times there is little to be seen, but diagrams at the site vividly portray the fort in its phases from the Stone to Iron Ages. A later entrance gateway was a particularly ingenious piece of work. To the north-east of the Park is Short Wood, a superb small wood of large beeches. Beyond Brockworth is Gloucester.

Gloucester does not actually lie within the AONB, being down in the Severn Vale below the Cotswold edge, though protected by two outliers of the hills — Robinswood Hill and Churchdown.

W
4m
1½h
ooo
*

Gloucester Docks

The city site is an ancient one, probably earlier than the Roman city of *Glevum* — built here at a crossing point of the Severn, as the western bastion of early Roman efforts to subdue the tribesmen of Wales. There have been major excavations of this important Roman city, and finds can be seen in the City Museum. In addition, and in keeping with the city's decision to retain its past as part of a lively present, the excavations of the Roman city's Eastgate (in Eastgate Street), has been opened up close to the main shopping precinct. Here a glass-topped plinth set at street level allows a view of the remains below street level. At certain times the underground excavation itself can be viewed. Around the corner from Eastgate, in Brunswick Road, is the City Museum containing finds from the Roman excavations and other items of local interest, such as the Birdlip mirror.

Gloucester remained an important city when the Romans had been replaced by the Saxons, not only because of its position on the Severn, but because it stood on the boundary of Mercia and Wessex, two of the three great Saxon kingdoms of England. The Cotswolds themselves represented a high-level route between the kingdoms, jealously guarded because of its strategic importance, and as a garrison city Gloucester was critical. Its importance can be gauged by the many centres for monastic life created there. Several Saxon rulers endowed convents or

monasteries, and the Mercian king
Aethelred, brother of Alfred the Great,
brought the body of St Oswald from
Lincolnshire here and founded a priory
around the tomb. The remains of the
priory, or at least those of the Norman
modifications to the original building,
can still be seen to the north of the
cathedral.

There was a Saxon royal palace near
the priory, and Aethelred was buried
here. Certainly at that stage Gloucester
was the central city of Mercia and the
only city comparable with Winchester,
the capital of Wessex. When England
was finally united against the Danes,
power shifted to the east and to London,
the capital accepted by the Norman
conquerors. But Gloucester remained

important, early Norman kings holding
a council here in the autumn of each
year. Indeed it was here, in the chapter
house of the cathedral, that William the
Conqueror drew up his plans for the
Domesday Book. The chapter house is
the oldest surviving part of the
cathedral, one of the most
architecturally important buildings in
Britain, a fine, and early, example of the
Perpendicular style of architecture.
Within, there is a treasury of fine work.
The cloisters are one of the few surviving
examples of this most obvious feature of
monastic life. They are roofed by
marvellous fan-vaulting, and include the
monks' lavatory, or wash-house, on one
side. The very ancient east window is the
largest of any British cathedral,

constructed to commemorate victory at the battle of Crecy. The cathedral is the only site apart from Westminster Abbey to have been used for a Coronation for over 700 years; Henry III was crowned here — as a nine-year-old, and with his mother's bracelet — a few days after the death of King John. The Coronation was a hasty move — John had been dead only nine days — to avoid civil war, and was carried out here to avoid the delay of a journey to London. The tomb of Edward II, murdered at Berkeley Castle, is in the north ambulatory.

Facing the cathedral is a memorial to Bishop Hooper, burnt at the stake here in 1555 for being a Lutheran. He spent the night before his execution in a half-timbered building in Westgate Street.

The building, a beautiful three-storeyed house with double over-hangs, is now known as Bishop Hooper's Lodgings and contains a folk museum, which has a replica of a wheelwright's shop.

A little less than 100 years later there was more fire and death in the city when the Parliamentarian govenor Sir Edward Massey was besieged by a Royalist army under the king himself. At that time the city stood between the King's capital at Oxford and his main support in Wales, and its occupation was vital to both sides. The graphic contemporary account of the siege includes one of the earliest records of the bombardment of civilians — 'they also shoot from the same battery (outside the City) above 20 fiery melting hot iron bullets some 18lbs.

*The Robert Opie Collection,
Gloucester*

others 20lbs. weight. In the night we perceived them flying in the air liking star-shooting. . . One came through three houses and fell into a chamber of Mr Cameline, the apothecary, and being perceived, many pails of water were cast upon it to quench the same but, that little availing, it was cast into a bowle of water where after a good space it cooled.'

When eventually a relief army arrived, the city was down to its last three barrels of powder, and the king withdrew. Puritan supporters were so pleased that a rhyme was constructed for Massey:

He that doth stand so well upon his guard
I hope shall never miss a good reward

and includes, in the last five words, an anagram of his name rendered as Edward Massie Governor.

Gloucester as a port and a centre for light industry, has continued to prosper, but its past history is recalled in a fine series of reliefs on buildings in the city centre. Another place of interest is the Tailor of Gloucester's house, a Beatrix Potter Museum, the one actually used as the model for the book and containing scenes from it. There is a Brass Rubbing Centre at the cathedral, where visitors may rub replicas from many churches. In Commercial Road, at the southern end of Southgate Street, is the Regimental Museum of the Glosters, opened in 1980 and containing relics from their campaigns.

Two further monastic remains are Blackfriars, founded in the early thirteenth century, which contains, in the church, a superb roof from that time; and Greyfriars, a sixteenth-century building near the new covered market. There are also a number of fine, mainly Norman, churches, and many beautiful houses. Any walk around Gloucester is worthwhile. Those who would prefer a more formal guided tour can join one at St Michael's Tower at the junction of the four 'gate' streets.

80

6 The Valleys Around Stroud _____

This section of the Cotswolds includes the Stroud Valley, the most heavily industrialised area in the region, and the wooded valleys on each side that drain into it. In earlier times the name Cotswold was applied only to that area of land around the headwaters of the Windrush, but gradually it was extended to more and more land to the south that was similar in geography and agriculture. By the latter part of the last century the name meant all land down to the Stroud Valley. More recently the area has been extended again to include the land south of Stroud. Geologically, the Cotswolds extend to Bath, but there is a change in geography, the wolds of the north being replaced by the lower

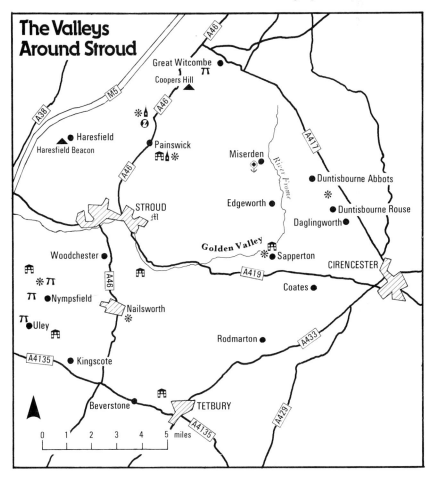

The Valleys Around Stroud

wooded land of the south. Stroud represents the transitional region between the two.

The change is exemplified by the wooded escarpment around Birdlip, north of Painswick. Before seeking the woody seclusion, one should go along to Barrow Wake, a steep bare part of the escarpment on the A417, just a little south of the Air Balloon Inn on the junction of the road with the A436, where there is a memorial to Peter Hopkins, 'Geologist and Christian'. It is a fine memorial, but it also has a portrait of the local area in the rock that comprises each section. The visitor can therefore not only enjoy the expansive view, but also have the differing rock types pointed out. To the right is the edge of Crickley Hill, with the clear escarpment outcrop. To the left is The Peak, the final promontory of Birdlip Hill, and beyond that, a section of wooded escarpment that forms the Witcombe Estate. Below are the villages of Great and Little Witcombe, and Gloucester cathedral beyond. Further on, the River Severn meanders its way around the Arlingham Bend in front of the Forest of Dean. At the northern end of the forest May Hill may be seen, its summit distinctively topped with a crown of trees.

Birdlip sits at the top of the escarpment, known here as Birdlip Hill. Those approaching the village from the Witcombe villages up the hill itself will see just how steep the escarpment can be. Beneath the wooded hill and the Peak are the remains of an Iron Age hillfort where excavations unearthed the finest collection of Iron Age jewellery so far discovered in Britain. It includes the Birdlip Mirror, a unique object, made around 50BC. It is a 6in diameter flat bronze disc with a 3in handle, made by the lost wax system, skillfully engraved and inlaid with red enamel. It can be seen in Gloucester Museum.

Witcombe Wood forms one of the best long wood walks in the Cotswolds. It follows a section of the Cotswold Way, from Birdlip to Cooper's Hill. A good return from here is to drop down the valley, and go between the reservoirs to Great Witcombe, although this involves a steep climb back to Birdlip.

W
6m
2½h
oo
*

Cooper's Hill is famous for its cheese rolling competition which takes place annually at the Spring Holiday. Contestants chase 7lb cheeses down the slope and anyone catching a cheese keeps it. The slope is sometimes fenced off to avoid erosion, but the healthy visitor can reach the maypole at the top by going through the trees at the side. Looking down it is easy to see why few people ever actually catch the cheese, and why minor injuries and concussions are frequent. The maypole is too close to the edge for dancing, but it is a reminder that the celebration once also included wrestling, dancing and singing.

Near the cheese rolling slope is Witcombe Roman Villa. Though not in the class of Chedworth, and not containing anything to equal the Woodchester pavement, it is nonetheless interesting.

In the woods above the cheese rolling slope — known collectively as Cranham Woods, although that name is strictly only applicable to those near Cranham village, others being Brockworth Wood and Buckholt Wood — there are a number of nature trails with colour-coded, signposted ways and information boards that cross the Cooper's Hill Nature Reserve. **Cranham** village is, as one would expect, close to woodland, but on its southern side there is an area of common. It is difficult to be too enthusiastic about the woodland around the village — it is one of the finest woods in Britain and is spectacular in autumn as the leaves change colour. Any walk from Cranham is worthwhile, and with Birdlip and Cooper's Hill only 1½ miles east and west, and the pleasant hamlet of Sheepscombe also 1½ miles away to the south, there is no shortage of excellent routes.

W
3m
1h
ooo
*

A little way from Cranham, on a pleasant site halfway down the

82

*Bellringing at Prinknash
Abbey*

Prinknash Abbey

escarpment, overlooking the Gloucester Vale, is Prinknash Abbey. The name is not pronounced as written, but as 'Prinage'. The abbey is not an ancient and historic building, but modern — a little too modern perhaps — and looking in no way like an abbey. The visitor is immediately struck by the colour of the stone, but it *is* Cotswold. It was quarried in the Guiting Quarry not far from the Cotswold Farm Park, though it will need a few hundred years to mellow into the countryside. The visitor has limited access to the abbey itself, which is Benedictine, and can also visit the world-famous pottery, where the monks, with lay craftsmen, throw, decorate and fire their distinctive range of pottery.

The Prinknash Bird Park, set in about 10 acres of parkland that form part of the original Prinknash estate, contains a large number of birds, mainly geese and pheasants, free and free-flying in natural surroundings. There is also a pets' corner where some exotic species of sheep and goats keep company with the usual assortment of children's pets.

Further south towards Stroud is **Painswick**, a gem of a village, almost a small town, with an interesting and long history. The visitor who braves the iron shots on the local golf course to reach the top of Painswick Beacon sees not only an expansive view, but also the ditches and ramparts of an ancient hillfort. This pre-dates the town by several centuries, but the village had a lord in Norman times. A later lord was

W
1m
½h
ooo
*

Painswick

the infamous and callous Sir Anthony Kingston, who appears to have had a genius for cruelty.

Henry VIII came here with Anne Boleyn for a couple of happy days' holiday, but within twelve months the happiness had faded, and Anne Boleyn was led out by her jailer for execution; the jailer was Anthony Kingston's father. Sir Anthony was a friend of King Henry, a friendship based, in part, on Kingston's willingness to carry out certain unpleasant tasks with enthusiasm. He put down a northern rebellion following the Dissolution of Monasteries with much enthusiasm, and later did the same in Bodmin. There he excelled himself by accepting the mayor's hospitality and then escorting

him to a set of gallows rapidly constructed by the mayor's men at his command, but on Kingston's orders. 'Thinke you, Mister Maior, that they be strong inough' asked Kingston. 'Yea, sir, that they are' replied the Mayor, anxious to please. 'Well then get you even up unto them, for they are provided for you,' 'and so without respit or staie there was the maior hanged'.

Sir Anthony also officiated in Gloucester at the burning of Bishop Hooper. In the Painswick area he had a gallows erected and men paid to be ready to put it to instant use. Not surprisingly, he was hated in the town, to such an extent, that when the church was later damaged during the Civil War, the locals used it as a cover for their own

Court House, Painswick
Fine early seventeenth-century
house with panelled room

Daneway House
Fine small Cotswold manor
dating, in part, from the
fourteenth century

Miserden Park
Spring bulbs and rose gardens

Painswick House
Fine Palladian mansion with good
original decor including Chinese
wallpaper

Smerrill Farm Museum
Historical collection of farm and
country craft tools housed in a
typical Cotswold farm

Town and District Museum, Stroud
Collections on local history.
Display of fossils including a 20ft
dinosaur

Witcombe Roman Villa
Excellent excavated remains of
well-sited small villa

Thameshead, Coates
Source of River Thames

Bird Park, Prinknash Abbey
Free-flying birds including snow-
geese. Also pygmy goats and
Haunted Monk's Pond.

Wildfowl Trust, Slimbridge
Sir Peter Scott's original site.
Famous for its migratory geese
and swans, but including captive
species

Duntisbourne Leer
Road along the bed of the stream

Frampton-on-Severn
Largest village green in England

Town Stocks, Painswick

Painswick Church
Fine collection of yew trees and
table-top tombs

Severn Bore
Tidal race, best seen at
Stonebench

Prinknash Abbey and Pottery
Modern abbey with limited access
for the visitor. Famous pottery
can be visited and there is a site
shop

vandalising of his elaborate tomb.
Painswick church makes a good start
to a walk around the town. It is a fine
building, but the churchyard is
interesting, too. The yews are steeped in
legend. One version has it that they
cannot be counted, while another says
that there are ninety-nine trees and that
if a hundreth is planted, it dies. The
churchyard path below the yews thread

through the very famous collection of
table-top tombs: there are, indeed, two
guides to tomb trails.
At the south end of the churchyard,
just beyond the wall, are the town
stocks, and a set of leg-irons; to the side
of these is the Court House, a superb
early seventeenth century house built for
a clothier, but named from a later owner
who was a lawyer. From here the walker

passes on the right the vicarage, a delightful house. Further on, through Friday Street, is Bisley Street. On the right, are a group of houses that date from the fourteenth century — the Chur, Little Fleece, and Wickstone. There is even an original arched packhorse doorway for deliveries to the rear of the buildings, parts of which were an inn. Straight on from here, and adding one mile to the walk is Painswick House, another fine house built in the eighteenth and nineteenth centuries in the style of Palladio. The interior is elegantly decorated and includes a room with Chinese wallpaper. Left from The Chur is New Street, in which there is a beautiful timbered house, now the Post Office. The foreign tourist regards such houses as essentially English, but here in the Cotswolds the buildings seem almost out of place. Further down the street is the Falcon Hotel, an eighteenth century inn, that was once the scene of cock fights between Painswick and neighbouring towns.

Further down the Painswick valley is **Pitchcombe**, a tiny hamlet on the A4173 still almost secluded in spite of the road. It has a delightful manor house and a fine old mill house. Above Pitchcombe is Edge, another pretty hamlet with a name that is explicit in terms of its position, for the road that leads to **Harescombe**, in the Vale below, seems to fall off the edge. The valley floor from Harescombe to **Haresfield** has the distinction of being the only section of the Cotswolds AONB that lies at the foot of the western escarpment. The two villages retain a Cotswold appearance — Harescombe Grange is an elegant manor house with good views of the river — but lose something in being away from the Wolds or out of a wooded, steep valley. In Haresfield church is a poignant epitaph by Dryden to an 11-year-old boy that ends with the couplet:

> knowing Heaven his home, to shun delay
> He leap'd o'er age and took the shortest way.

To regain the Cotswolds from Haresfield the visitor must tackle the escarpment slope again, and it is long and steep. At the top is Haresfield Beacon, perhaps the finest viewpoint for the escarpment itself, and a good spot from which to see the Berkeley Vale, as the lower Severn Vale is known. The actual tip of the escarpment, which has a triangulation pillar, is reached by following the Cotswold Way from the top of the hill from Haresfield. The view takes in the sweep of Standish Wood, then Frocester Hill, the other side of the Stroud Valley, and Cam Long Down and Stinchcombe Hill (the most westerly point of the Cotswolds) above Dursley. In good weather one can glimpse the Severn Bridge.

The panorama is a little less expansive but better signed for the mapless, at the topograph, a mile or so from the beacon. One can reach this by following the Cotswold Way again, reversing the outward route and continuing east. Beyond the topograph is Standish Wood, an excellent piece of woodland with numerous tracks. Beyond are Randwick and Whiteshill, villages on the side of the Stroud valley.

East of Painswick the area is again characterised by steep-sided valleys each carrying a stream. The first of these is the Slad valley, famous for its association with Laurie Lee's book *Cider with Rosie*. Many of the places mentioned in the book can be identified — Steanbridge, a modified Elizabethan house, is the squire's house. The valley and road starts above **Sheepscombe**, although this village is actually at the head of the Painswick valley. These two valleys were among the most important mill valleys in the Cotswolds at the height of the wool trade, as can be seen by the number of mills that line the tiny streams. Sheepscombe was too high to benefit from water power, but its name recalls the other element of a successful wool industry; the village was the site of Sir Anthony Kingston's gallows.

Above Sheepscombe the B4070 runs

W
1m
½h
ooo
*

W
1m
½h
ooo
*

86

View south to Cotswold Edge and Severn Vale from Haresfield Beacon

between the Painswick and Slad valleys, dropping down into the latter below Bulls Cross. It is a delightful road in these upper regions. At Bulls Cross there is a good view across to Painswick; further down, the valley closes in on each side.

The next valley to the east is the Toadsmoor, with a stream that flows down from **Bisley**. The village, high and unprotected, is a bleak place in winter, recalling the northern high wold villages. It has a very ancient six-sided memorial, with seats that cover what was elegantly called a bone hole, where heaps of bones were dumped when old graves were broken open. It is said that around 600 years ago the priest fell into it one night and died; when the Pope was informed, he was so angry that he ordered, as punishment, that there should be no burials for two years. Instead the villagers trekked 15 miles to Bibury to bury their dead in 'Bisley piece'. The route, known as Dead Man's Lane, can still, in theory be followed past the

Giant's Stone. Here, 'men have had the terrifying experience of seeing headless human beings which have now vanished'. In fact this stone is all that remains of a long barrow. The many stones in the area all seem to be associated with similar legends. The name Money Tump, also said to have been haunted by headless men, suggests a treasure site, and another barrow nearer Oakridge, to the south, stands in Golden Coffin Field, so named from the belief that a golden coffin was buried here. The ghost stories were probably invented by field owners to keep strangers away while they searched for buried treasure.

All around Bisley there are delightful, isolated, sheltered hamlets. Any of the minor roads from Bisley give rewarding walks and the valley stream can be followed to Eastcombe, the last village before the descent into the Stroud valley.

The Frome Valley actually becomes the Stroud valley as the Frome flows on to the Severn. In its lower reaches,

Sapperton Tunnel Portal

between Chalford and Stroud, it is called the Golden Valley. In its upper reaches the Frome is in a truly golden valley, particularly in autumn when the woodland that covers the steep sides turns copper-gold. The river rises at **Brimpsfield**, only a little south of Birdlip, where there are the remains of a castle built about 700 years ago by John Gifford, a descendant of one of William the Conqueror's captains. Unfortunately when Gifford opposed Edward II, his castle was slighted. The local people plundered the castle for building stone and so now only the foundations and ditches, or moats, survive. The portcullis grooves on stones near the entrance can just be discerned.

From Brimpsfield the descent to **Caudle Green** is steep, but there the motorist has to stop. The road is never continuous, making occasional darts down into the valley to cross it, from the top of each valley side. Below Caudle Green is Miserden, with its park and well-known gardens. The beautifully situated mansion is Elizabethan, but only the park is open to visitors. A visit is best made in the spring when the bulbs are out, but the rock gardens can be enjoyed at any time of the year.

From Miserden to Edgeworth the road again leaves the valley floor, but the walker can find a way there by lane and path. **Edgeworth** itself has a fine manor house, seen particularly well from the road into the valley from Duntisbourne Leer.

At **Daneway**, two miles further down river from Edgeworth, the house, which dates in part from around 1250, is open to visitors who have made an appointment. There have been numerous additions, all in the style of the corresponding age, and earlier this century it was used as a furniture and craft workshop by Sidney and Ernest Barnsley and Ernest Gimson.

Also at Daneway is an inn which stands near the entrance to Sapperton Tunnel, which formed part of the Thames and Severn Canal and was, at 3,817yd, the longest ever built in Britain at the time of its completion in 1789. It was constructed by digging shafts from the surface to the correct depth and tunnelling outwards in each direction. The work was carried out by 'navvies' — the name for those who constructed 'navigations'. The tunnel was 15ft in diameter, bricked where needed, and the boats were pushed through by the boatmen lying on their backs and walking on the tunnel roof.

The tunnel is named from **Sapperton**, a larger village slightly closer to the canal tunnel entrance. It is a pretty village, well situated at the end of the Broad Ride from Cirencester Park, and on the side of the Frome Valley. It also stands at the crossroads between the old agricultural uplands and the industrial lowlands. The division is exemplified not only by the Sapperton Tunnel, but also by the tunnel that took the trains from Gloucester to Paddington — it was started down the valley from Sapperton, actually a little closer to the village of Frampton Mansell, a small place, not as pretty as Sapperton, with a romantic name. From there it was driven just over a mile towards the canal tunnel, at a gradient of 1 in 90 up and, later, 1 in 93 down. The railway passes over the canal tunnel about 1½ miles west of Coates village.

Leaving Sapperton and its tunnel, one can follow the Duntisbourne valley, which drains into the Churn at Cirencester. It is characterised not by the steeply wooded slopes of the Slad and the Frome, but by a collection of fine villages. The first, **Winstone**, a hamlet of a few houses, straggles for almost a mile along a minor road that links Caudle Green to Ermin Way, the A417.

From here a walk, by pathway and lane, leads past all the Duntisbourne villages to Daglingworth. **Duntisbourne Abbots** is the first. It is built down the valley side, but terraced so well that the visitor at the base of the slope can see all the houses and the church high above. It is a place of considerable charm, a

V
2m
³/₄h
o
**

V
4m
1½h
oo
**

89

Duntisbourne Leer

charm enhanced by the fact that between Duntisbourne Abbots and Duntisbourne Leer the road goes along the stream bed: or perhaps the stream goes over the road. The likely explanation for this is that carts and horses emerging from this section of the road might have clean wheels and hooves. Perhaps it was, in part, a cart dip, used to expand wooden wheels and spokes and so tighten the joints. **Duntisbourne Leer** is, like so many other villages, named from the abbey that was awarded the manor in early medieval times. The difference is that the abbey was not in England at all, but at Lire, in Normandy. There are fords at **Middle Duntisbourne** and at **Duntisbourne Rouse**, but neither is as good as the Leer ford. Rouse has a beautiful church, probably with considerable Saxon work, on the hill above the hamlet. In the churchyard there is a fourteenth-century cross with a very long shaft. Over the ford here and up the hill towards the A417 is a small

workshop where garden furniture is made from Cotswold stone. The visitor can also buy a miniature staddle stone, a nice souvenir, typical of the Cotswolds.

The final village, **Daglingworth**, has a church that is an even finer piece of Saxon work than that at Duntisbourne Rouse. The interior includes three rare Saxon pre-conquest sculptures, and the tomb of Giles Handcox, a definite pragmatist. The tomb contains his 'dissection and distribution' and the inscription states that the man wished the earth to have his remains, heaven his soul, his friends his love, and the local poor £5 for their 'best advantage and releefe'. Further down river from the church and main village is another section of the village, the Lower End. Here is the manor house, with a medieval circular dovecote and its rotating ladder that allowed access to the nesting sites. This dovecote has over 500 nest holes.

South from here is **Coates**, a tiny

90

*Duntisbourne Rouse
Church*

straggling village that has not only the railway and the exit from the Sapperton tunnel, but also the accepted source of the Thames within its parish boundary. All three can be seen from one walk. If the walker starts from Coates, the Portal pub near the canal tunnel makes a fine staging post. A 1½ mile extension includes **Tarlton**, a hamlet that contains thatched cottages.

Beyond Tarlton is **Rodmarton**, a pleasant upland village with prehistoric and Roman sites in its surroundings. The A433, which leaves the Foss Way for Culkerton at the quaintly-named Jackaments Bottom, lies in a wooded valley below Rodmarton, and on the far side of the valley is Kemble airfield. This has the Foss Way running right through its centre.

Kemble is also the site of the Smerrill Farm Museum which contains the the Clement Collection of historical farming implements.

Culkerton and nearby **Ashley** are exposed, but charming, hamlets. Ashley has a manor house that dates, in part, from the fifteenth century. West of Rodmarton, **Cherington** is at the head of another valley that flows down into the Stroud valley. The village itself has dignified houses around a green on which is a drinking fountain inscribed 'let him that is athirst, come'.

Next is **Avening**, a larger village that typifies more the industrialised Stroud valley. South of Avening is Chavenage House, which is not near any village. The house, largely of the mid sixteenth century, is a fine example of the work of the period. Inside there are rooms called Cromwell's and Ireton's, commemorating the night when these two important Parliamentarians stayed here in 1648. Beyond Avening is **Nailsworth**, a town rather than a village, built at the junction of two valleys. The town represents the transition from the old, wool-based industry to more modern manufacture and the buildings are mainly less than 200 years old. Despite that, it has considerable charm and is well worth a walk. The visitor will soon discover that many of the side streets are very steep. Steepest of all is the aptly named Nailsworth Ladder which is 1 in 2 or 1 in 2½ — no one seems absolutely certain. The centre of the town is marked by a clock tower of 1951. It is also the War Memorial, and it is claimed that it was constructed in such a way that the sound of the chimes carried to the surrounding villages.

To the south of Nailsworth is **Horsley**, set on the side of the valley towards the town. Anyone toiling up the hill there, to see its fine collection of seventeenth-century houses, will have some sympathy for the local cyclists who, every year, race on a circuit that involves climbing this hill not once, but three times for juniors and six times for

W
4m
½h
)oo
**

𝔐

Berkeley Castle
Medieval castle with great hall, keep and dungeons. Scene of Edward II's murder. Good collection of furniture, paintings etc. Ornamental gardens

Chavenage House
Elizabethan manor house. Collection of seventeenth century tapestries

Owlpen Manor
Very beautiful manor with terraced gardens in wonderful position

Coaley Peak Picnic Site
Includes the Frocester Hill viewpoint and Nympsfield long barrow

Frocester Tithe Barn
Sixteenth-century tithe barn and gate and court houses

Hetty Pegler's Tump
Superb chambered long barrow

Uleybury Hillfort
Large hillfort with still visible defences

Nailsworth Ladder
An exceptionally steep rough road out of the town

Minchinhampton Market House
seventeenth-century wool market house

seniors. Above Horsley, open wold land is reached again, on the far side of which is Kingscote, famous now not so much for its park and late Georgian house but for the excavations carried out at the extensive Roman settlement just the other side of the A4135.

To the north of Nailsworth is the land above the Stroud valley, and the valley itself. Gatcombe Park, a late eighteenth-century house, is now the residence of Princess Anne and Captain Mark Phillips. Gatcombe is a little north of Avening, and west of it is **Minchinhampton**, a fine village with a golf course laid out on one of the largest areas of common land south of Cleeve Hill. The common also shows the remains of a rampart and ditch system called The Bulwarks. This is an apt name for an Iron Age hillfort that defends an area of over 600 acres. North of this, at Rodborough, is a further area of common.

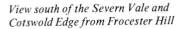

The Stroud or Golden Valley is a typical light industrial valley, but **Stroud** itself is a pleasant town. There is a Sports and Leisure Centre at Stratford Park, with good park walks and a pleasant lake on the complex. The town museum is a fascinating place with exhibits of local archaeology and the textile industry, as well as some surprising objects.

The Avon flows into the Frome below Stroud, and between it and the escarpment is **Woodchester**, a tiny village full of surprises. The first surprise is that it has seen not one but two monasteries, for Dominican and Franciscan monks. The second surprise is that nothing is really visible of one of the most famous British Roman villas. Here was discovered the Orpheus pavement, 2,210sqft in area containing $1\frac{1}{2}$ million $\frac{1}{2}$ inch cubes, the largest mosaic in Britain and one of the finest Roman remains outside Rome itself. Sadly, it is

not shown to the public. A full-sized replica can be seen at Wotton-under-Edge. Above Woodchester the escarpment is rejoined at Selsley Common, an ideal picnic spot. Better views are to be found further south, from Frocester Hill, where there is a panorama dial. In **Frocester** village, below the hill, is a superb tithe barn, open to the public. Near the panorama dial is the Coaley Peak Picnic Site. It has numerous charts to help identify the local animal and plant life and the Nympsfield long barrow whose name derives from the village a little way from the edge, nestling in a fold of the hills. The Bristol and Gloucestershire Gliding Club is at the top of Frocester Hill. There are conventional gliders, hang gliders and radio-controlled model gliders flying from here.

Hetty Pegler's Tump is a long barrow set away from the B4066 at the very edge of the escarpment. It is virtually intact and the visitor can only wonder at the dry stone walling of the 'horns' that protect the entrance. The art has changed little, if at all, in 4,000 years. The visitor is well rewarded, for although the doorway is low and the interior dark and wet, it is an unforgettable experience. To complete a tour of the better historical monuments of the area, the visitor can then visit Uleybury, a large well-protected hillfort formed around a promontory of the escarpment. The area enclosed is about 30 acres and the fort is probably the best on the Cotswolds.

The village of **Uley** sits below the fort; below the village itself, in a valley to the east, is **Owlpen**, a tiny hamlet with perhaps, the most delightful of all Cotswold manor houses. It is not an elaborate building; a straightforward three-gabled house, it does not have an architectural wholeness, parts dating

93

Nympsfield Long Barrow

Owlpen Manor

from the fifteenth to the eighteenth centuries. But it possesses an elegance of line and a simple beauty, enhanced by the yew trees on the lawns in front of it, and by a simple church and dense woodland in the background. No single view so typifies the beauty of the Cotswolds better than Owlpen in spring when the daffodils are in full colour.

Owlpen is the perfect finale for this section of the Cotswolds, but there is much in the vale below the edge that is worthy of note. At Slimbridge is Sir Peter Scott's Wildfowl Trust with its flocks of wild geese and swans, together with numerous specimens of wildfowl from all over the world. Frampton-on-Severn has the largest village green in England. At Arlingham the Severn swings through 180⁰ in two right-angled bends only a short distance apart giving the land around the village the feeling of being an island. The Severn Bore becomes noticeable at Arlingham, although it is at Stonebench, a few miles further up-river, that it reaches its peak.

94

7 The Southwolds

The part of the Cotswolds that lies between the M4 and the A4135 is, correctly, termed the Southwolds, and in this area the change in character that was apparent in the villages above Stroud becomes much more distinct. To the east, towards Tetbury, there are still acres of Wold land, but the countryside is now much softer, with the distinctive feature being the 'Bottoms', as the valleys around Wotton-under-Edge are known.

Tetbury is the largest town in the area, and it maintains much of the delightful character of a Cotswold market town of the seventeenth and eighteenth centuries. Its actual history is much longer. In the Civil War between Stephen and Matilda in the mid-twelfth century, Malmesbury, the local and important abbey town, was besieged. The besieging army set up base at Tetbury, called a 'castle only three miles distant'. The 'castle' may have been only a defensive earthwork, but Tetbury must have been of some note.

The town's position on, rather than beneath, the Wolds, prevented its being a great milling centre during the wool industry boom, but its central position allowed it to become a very prosperous market town. This had advantages at the time of the decline of the woollen industry, when the small industries that grow up around markets helped to keep the town solvent. Its proserity was also

The Market Hall, Tetbury

95

helped by being its own lord of the manor; the town bought the manor from Lord Berkeley, its last lord, in the early seventeenth century. It was then governed by a council of local yeomen, who were able to increase its prosperity by ploughing back any profits. The construction of the market hall in 1655 was an early expression of the place's prosperity.

To see the town it is best to walk, and there is a good starting point at the church of St Mary. This is a comparatively late church for the Cotswolds; there was no great wool-stapling family here. Built in a curious style, with huge windows that light up the interior, it has an interesting collection of large monuments, including one to the Saunders family,

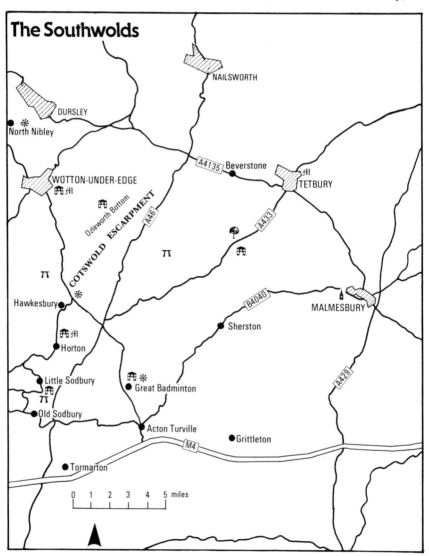

The Southwolds

NAILSWORTH

DURSLEY

North Nibley

WOTTON-UNDER-EDGE

Ozleworth Bottom

COTSWOLD ESCARPMENT

A46

A4135 Beverstone

TETBURY

A433

Hawkesbury

Horton

Little Sodbury

Old Sodbury

Great Badminton

Acton Turville

B4040

MALMESBURY

Sherston

Grittleton

A429

M4

Tormarton

0 1 2 3 4 5 miles

Owlpen Manor

Easton Grey

Somerset Monument

Castle Combe

but to which of its members?

In a vault underneath
lie several of the Saunderses
late of this parish; particulars
the Last Day will disclose

In Newchurch Street there is St Saviour's church, later than St Mary's. Apparently the parish church had few pews, and these were in the main bought by the town's rich merchants, to the exclusion of the poor. This idea of buying, or endowing, pews was not unique to Tetbury, but the idea of building a second church to accommodate the poor certainly is.

Walking from St Mary's down towards The Green one passes, at the far end to the right, Barton Abbots, a

Chipping Steps, Tetbury

97

Tetbury

beautiful three-storeyed house. On the left is Silver Street and one then reaches the Market Place. To the right is the Talbot Hotel which is mainly seventeenth century, but with later additions. The Market Hall, as noted earlier, was built in 1655. Considered one of the finest buildings of its type in the Cotswolds, it was once even better, for in 1817 it was 'renovated', being reduced by one storey and re-roofed; an end was filled, to provide the town with a lock-up, and to house the fire engine. The town's coat of arms is on the building. Opposite the Market Hall is the Snooty Fox, formerly called the White Hart Inn, a seventeenth-century building in Jacobean style. The inn stands in the corner of Chipping Lane which leads to The Chipping. The name, as mentioned previously, is the old word for a market; here the original market was held. From it the Chipping Steps, which are very old, lead down to Cirencester Road. Near them, The

Priory contains part of the old monastery buildings.

The walker can now return to the church by going along Church Street; The Close is a beautiful three-storeyed four-gabled house a little way up Long Street; or he can go along Long Street, down Newchurch Street, passing St Saviour's and turn left into West Street. In Long Street, at the Old Court House, is a most unusual museum, the Police Bygones Museum which houses a collection of articles on the history of the Gloucestershire Constabulary.

South from Tetbury the A433 runs past an estate that has recently achieved fame — Highgrove. The house, built in the last few years of the eighteenth century, had to be extensively restored a century later when it was gutted by fire. The lodge remains from the original construction. Prince Charles and the Princess of Wales now live there.

Further along the A433 is the hamlet of **Westonbirt**. Its famous school is housed in Westonbirt Manor, a mid-nineteenth-century mansion set in park land elegantly laid out with lawns and trees. The school itself is not open to the public, but the gardens can be visited by prior appointment.

The village has a famous Arboretum covering over 100 acres with perhaps the finest collection of trees in Britain, including the Redwood; although the specimen here does not approach the height of those in California, it does give some idea of the spectacular nature of those giants. The tree has a very strange bark, not hard as on most British trees, but soft and fibrous, and a rich chestnut in colour. The Arboretum, set up by Robert Holford, whose alabaster effigy can be seen in the village church, is now managed by the Forestry Commission. Visitors in the Autumn are assured of one of the most colourful sights in the Cotswolds, while those who come in the spring can see a spectacular show of rhododendrons and azaleas.

Those not overwhelmed by trees can walk along the bridlepath in Silk Wood a little way south of the Arboretum, or can skirt the wood to the north-east. Either route emerges on to a track across open country, and the return to the main road is by a lane from Leighterton. The village itself can be visited if the walk is extended by 1½ miles.

To the south of Westonbirt, sandwiched between the A433 and the Foss Way, is a small area of the Cotswolds through which flows the River Avon. Here the Cotswold boundary is again the Foss Way, and the best route to explore these Avon villages is to follow the river and return along the Foss Way itself. But first is **Shipton Moyne**, a tiny village of grey stone, memorable for the three fourteenth century monuments in the church — two knights in armour, the third a lady, each in a canopied recess with elaborate decorations.

The walk along the Avon starts at Easton Grey and takes a path on the south bank to Sherston Parva and Sherston itself. From there the south bank is again followed towards

W
5m
1¾h
o
**

Westonbirt Arboretum

99

Luckington. Then there is a lane towards Alderton and to the Foss Way at Foss Lodge. The Way can then be followed all the way back to the river near Easton Grey. This very long walk can be reduced by about 5 miles by reaching the Foss Way directly from Sherston. This omits Luckington, a pretty village near the actual source of the Avon. **Sherston** is a pleasant village, well-situated and associated with the legend of John Rattlebones, who, with Edmund Ironsides, is said to have defeated the Danes near here in 1016. The church contains an effigy known as Rattlebones; but as it is Norman, it is far more likely to be a saint than a Saxon general. The last village, **Easton Grey**, is the best: there is a fine Georgian mansion, and an arched bridge over the Avon. There are fine views of the river from here. Beyond Easton Grey the Avon leaves the Cotswolds. The visitor to Malmesbury sees it again, and it reappears at Bath, by which time it is a fine river on its way to the sea beyond Bristol.

Malmesbury lies to the east of the Foss Way, and outside the AONB. It is also distinctly non-Cotswold, the Wiltshire market towns having their own atmosphere. It is worthy of a visit, however, with superb remains of the abbey.

Back on the A433 is the village of **Didmarton**, near the source of the Avon. Like Tetbury, Didmarton also has two churches. Here the Victorians, who vandalised many Cotswold churches, decided that it was cheaper to build a new one. The lover of churches will be delighted, because the older building is unspoilt — with a fine triple-decker pulpit.

From here a good walk is to follow the track to Oldbury-on-the-Hill, and the bridleway beyond to Nan Tow's Tump. It is difficult to make the return by a different route unless one is willing to risk travelling along the A46, but it is only two miles in any case.

Oldbury-on-the-Hill is a group of

cottages around a church dedicated to St Arild, a Saxon princess, but it has little as old. Much older is **Nan Tow's Tump**, which differs from all the barrows so far mentioned in being round, rather than long. It is the finest example of its type in the area and is 9ft high in the centre. Nan Tow was the name of a local witch who, legend has it, was buried upright in the mound as a punishment for her wickedness: again a supernatural aura surrounds a burial mound. In this case the locals took handfuls of earth from the mound as it was supposed to be a cure for many illnesses.

Beyond the Tump is **Leighterton**, a small village where six roads converge. The church here is a good example of the Victorian 'restoration' that has spoilt so many ancient churches. Here a beautiful hamlet church, dating from the thirteenth century, was restored almost beyond recognition 100 years ago.

At **Beverstone**, a couple of miles west

W
4m
1¼h
oo
*

100

of Tetbury, is a castle that is still occupied. Although not open to the public, it is visible from the roadside. The castle was besieged in the Civil War in 1644, by Colonel Massey and his Parliamentarian soldiers. The castle was held for the king by Colonel Oglethorpe. Oglethorpe provided stout resistance, and a frontal attack, supported by guns, was beaten back. Massey settled down for a long siege and Oglethorpe, expecting a few quiet hours, if not days and weeks, slipped out to visit his mistress on a neighbouring farm, with just a few soldiers for protection. Acting on information received, Massey visited the farm and Oglethorpe was captured. Massey then offered safe transit to Malmesbury for the defenders of the castle, on condition they left behind their weapons, and Oglethorpe's deputy accepted. Ironically, as soon as Massey had taken control of Beverstone he marched on Malmesbury and captured

it, taking prisoner all those who had been granted safe passage from the castle.

West of Beverstone, and west of the A46, is 'bottom' country, where deeply cut, wooded valleys split the wold right down through the escarpment. But before following a bottom down, one should stay on the wold a little longer. At **Lasborough** is a seventeenth-century manor which contains many excellent fireplaces, and a good collection of paintings and china. Equally interesting are the gardens with good borders and shrubberies. A little south-west is another fine house, Boxwell Court, beautifully situated in the wooded upper folds of Ozleworth Bottom. Charles II came here after the Battle of Worcester, although it is not clear whether he stayed. One version of the story has it that he did, accompanied by Matthew Huntley, owner of the Court. Another says that the king arrived without Huntley whose wife, fearful of his capture as the house had been searched several times in previous days, persuaded him to sleep in the barn of a nearby farm. In any case the king was grateful enough to Mrs Huntley to send her, from his hideout in France, a turquoise ring which is still in the family's possession.

Below Boxwell is **Ozleworth Bottom**. Its top is easy to locate for the British Telecom microwave transmitter above Ozleworth village is visible for many miles in all directions. The village is hardly a village at all, just a couple of farms around a park and a house of the eighteenth century. Within the private grounds of the house the visitor can reach the unusual church. A six-sided tower stands in the middle of the church, the only example in the Cotswolds and rare elsewhere: no sides are the same. The circular churchyard is also very unusual, and contains the grave of the last Englishman hanged for the crime of

Ozleworth Bottom

highway robbery. Below the church the road falls steeply a neat row of cottages — all that remains of a village which once housed 1,600 people. They lived here because the river, the Little Avon, that runs in the bottom was one of the strongest in the neighbourhood, and was the source of power for many mills in the area. Indeed when one looks at old maps of the area around Wotton it is astonishing just how many mills were working at the height of the woollen trade. A river such as this could have had more than one mill per mile.

Beyond the cottages the river can be followed back up into the wooded valley, although the route is not easily found. An easier route is to follow the lane down towards Wortley, but the walker needs to be met by car here to avoid having to retrace his steps, as the river bank is not a public right of way. The bottom is a delightful place, particularly in the upper reaches behind the cottages. In spring, when the flowers are blooming and the birds are nesting, there are few places as quiet and more

V
2m
³/₄h
ooo
**

relaxing. There are no unusual varieties of flowers, and the birds are common enough, but the setting adds a new beauty. The lucky visitor may also catch a glimpse of a pair of the famous Gloucestershire hares boxing in their madness. The Little Avon leaves the Cotswolds between Alderley and Wortley, small mill hamlets. **Alderley**, slightly the bigger, has a fine Elizabethan house that is now a boys' school. **Wortley** is now little more than a couple of cottages and a memory of past glories. Stephen Hopkins, who was born here, sailed on the *Mayflower* to the New World. Wortley is not, in fact, on the Little Avon, but on a tributary that flows in the quaintly named Nanny Farmer's Bottom.

North of Ozleworth is **Tyley Bottom** in which a stream, flowing down to **Wotton-under-Edge**, can be followed by a track for a mile above the town. Wotton is truly 'under-Edge', the escarpment looming above the northern and eastern sides of the town like a defensive wall. At the northern end it is

V
2m
³/₄h
oo
*

W
1m
½h
oo
*
T
1m
oo
*

called Wotton Hill, and a steep climb leads to a small enclosure of trees and a fine view of the town. In the town there is much of interest, and the walker will be well rewarded. In High Street is the Tolsey; it has been a courthouse, a lock-up, and a few other things in its time. It has a large, interesting clock and a weathervane shaped like a dragon. From it, Market Street leads to The Chipping, another use of the old word, and contains some fine, restored timber-framed houses. So good was the restoration that the street has received an architectural award. Further down High Street, Berkeley House had a room with green-painted pine panelling and Chinese wallpaper from the mid-eighteenth century; it was so fine that it was dismantled and moved complete to the Victoria and Albert Museum in London for permanent exhibition. Orchard Street contains the house in which Isaac Pitman lived while teaching in Wotton and where, it is believed, he first worked on his shorthand. At the bottom of High Street, on the left is Long Street, where the Perry Almshouses can be visited. The seventeenth-century facade gives way to a courtyard and a small, contemporary chapel — a quiet place. At the bottom of Long Street stood a grammar school founded in 1384 by Katherine, Lady Berkeley. Such a benefaction was remarkably early, and is commemorated in the name of the modern comprehensive school which stands outside the town.

Back in Long Street, a right turn takes the walker to the Ram Inn, a timbered house below road level, perhaps old enough to have been the actual one to house the masons who built the church: it is no longer an inn. The church itself is an elegant building and has a very famous memorial brass to Thomas, Lord Berkeley, and his wife Margaret. Lifesized and very old, it is probably pre-1400. Lord Berkeley was a remarkable man. He fought the Scots for Richard II; under Henry IV he was admiral of the fleet that defeated the French allies of Owen Glendower at Milford Haven; later he fought with

103

The Ram Inn, Wootton-under-Edge

Henry V at Agincourt. As was the custom of the time, his marriage to Lady Margaret was arranged very early in their lives. At the time of the wedding Thomas was probably 14, while Margaret was, at most, 7. She died at 30 having had one daughter. Thomas was grief-stricken, and never remarried for the remaining 25 years of his life. His lack of a male heir was the direct cause of the Battle of Nibley Green, the field of which can be seen a few miles north of Wotton. Rubbings from exact resin replicas of the brass can be made with permission of the church.

Another delightful reminder of long ago can be seen at the Rev Rowland Hill's Tabernacle Church in Tabernacle Road, which runs parallel to Gloucester Street. He was from the same family as the famous Postmaster General, and dominated Wotton's religious life in the years around 1770. He built the church and later moved to London. The church was recently acquired by Mr R. and Mr J. Woodward, who have painstakingly reconstructed a copy of the

Woodchester Roman pavement. Expert opinion was sought to fill in the missing sections of the original; this, however was later considered to be too fanciful and meaningless. It was dismantled in favour of a partial mosaic which is an exact replica of the remains of the original pavement. Also in the church are exhibits from the recent excavations at Kingscote. A little way south-west of Wotton and just outside the AONB is the village of **Kingswood**: it was the site of a Norman abbey. The abbey was demolished following dissolution, but its fifteenth-century gatehouse still remains, a fine old building which now houses the local council chamber — probably the oldest in Britain.

From Wotton the best way of continuing north is to follow a small section of the Cotswold Way through Westridge wood above the town to the Nibley Monument, returning along any of the wood's many paths. The wood itself, a delightful place, is criss-crossed with wide avenues, and so walking is easy. Within it there is an Iron Age

π

π

W
4m
1½h
ooo
*

104

hillfort, known as Brackenbury Ditches. It is overgrown, however, and the ditches and ramparts are difficult to find. A gateway can be made out, and the site has tremendous atmosphere.

Beyond the wood is the Tyndale Monument, erected in the last century to the memory of William Tyndale; he was born near here, perhaps at Stinchcombe or Cam. Tyndale was, at one time, tutor at Little Sodbury Manor, further south, but he had left the area before translating the Bible into English, an achievement for which he was burned at the stake. The monument stands on Nibley Knoll, above the village itself, which is a straggling place with a fine church; below this is Nibley Green, the site of the last true battle fought between private armies on English soil. The battle followed the death without a male heir of Lord Berkeley, whose memorial brass is at Wotton. Berkeley's daughter married the Earl of Warwick, but when the titles passed to his nephew, the succession was disputed by Warwick's children and eventually a great-grandson of Berkeley, Lord Lisle, challenged the new Lord Berkeley to a duel to decide the issue. This developed into a full scale battle between rival armies. Lord Lisle and several hundred others were killed, and his followers put to flight.

North Nibley sits at the head of Waterley Bottom which can be followed to the main road above Dursley, although there is no pathway. It is probably best to drive along a minor road to a point close to the top, and to walk down.

Dursley has been modernised to such an extent that little remains of the original Cotswold town. The market house still stands at the centre of the town, with a recessed statue of Queen Anne gazing across at the church. This commemorates the Queen's grant of cash to assist in the repair of the church following the collapse of the spire in 1698. It seems that the spire was in poor shape and was patched up with a

considerable quantity of lead and tiles. To celebrate completion of the work the bells were rung, and the vibration brought the spire down, killing several ringers.

In the past Dursley has produced gifted men, including Edward Fox, the Bishop of Hereford who introduced Cranmer to Henry VIII; and William King who has a stronger claim to having started the Sunday School movement than Robert Raikes in nearby Gloucester. Beyond Dursley is **Cam**, a small village with a still active flour mill, near a new housing estate. The village nestles below the hills of Peaked Down and Long Down, known locally as Cam Peak and Cam Long Down. The hills form a long ridged outlier of the Cotswold edge, and show its geological formation as rock has eroded back from the river. The peaks of harder, less easily weathered rock have been left behind. The two peaks can be climbed by following the Cotswold Way back from Home Farm. From the summit of Long Down there is a good view along the edge towards Frocester Hill. Cam Peak offers views to Dursley itself, and down the Berkeley Vale. Beyond Dursley can be seen Stinchcombe Hill, the most westerly point of the escarpment. The hill can be readily explored as it is the site of a golf course. It is in the shape of the letter T, very narrow near the club-house, and several hundred yards wide at the point — Drakestone Point. Its shape allows the walker to see right back into Waterley Bottom, and there are also excellent views along the Cotswold edge, both north and south.

West of Dursley, closer to the river Severn, **Berkeley** is a town of considerable interest. Berkeley Castle has been held by the same family for over 800 years. It is a beautiful building both outside and inside, with a long and interesting history, being famous as the site of the murder of Edward II. In the town is a museum to Edward Jenner who poineered vaccination against smallpox. Also west of Dursley, and

W
3m
1¼h
ooo
*

105

Horton Court

---

 near to Stinchcombe village, is the
Blanchworth Cider Mill: it still has the
original horse-drawn cider press, and is
now a gallery for local artists. Further
south, at Tortworth, is a 1,000 year old
chestnut tree which is almost 60ft round,
next to the church.

Returning to the Cotswold edge,
below Alderley is a string of villages
along the spring line, at the base of the
escarpment. **Hillesley** is a pleasant little
village near the Kilcott valley, which has
a delightful narrow country lane with a
stream flowing alongside it, and an old
mill near a calm, timeless mill pond.

The next village, **Hawkesbury**, has a
beautiful little church, with features
from many centuries, well-situated
beneath the wooded escarpment. Above
it is the Somerset, or Hawkesbury,
Monument. The tower commemorates
Lord Edward Somerset, a member of the
Beaufort family from nearby
Badminton. Lord Somerset served under
Wellington at Waterloo with such
gallantry that he received the official
thanks of Parliament. From the tower

there is a wonderful view back along the
edge, both the British Telecom tower at
Ozleworth, and the Tyndale monument
at North Nibley being visible. The view
southward is equally good, and on clear
days the mountains of Wales can be
seen. The monument stands on the
summit of the escarpment, and near to it
is **Hawkesbury Upton**, the 'Upton'
signifying its position. The most
noticeable feature of the village is,
perhaps, the pond, a large expanse of
water with a good number of ducks. On
the A46 just beyond the village are two
small hamlets, Dunkirk and Petty
France, whose names commemorate an
important landmark in the development
of the Cotswold woollen industry. In its
earliest days the wool was exported raw
to the continent, made into cloth and
then imported here. This was obviously
bad business, and an attempt was made
to encourage Flemish weavers to come
here. Crown agents were sent abroad to
extol the virtues of England, its good
beef, good living and 'good bedfellows!'
The two names indicate their success.

Somerset Monument, Hawksbury Upton

PLACES OF INTEREST AROUND
GREAT BADMINTON

Badminton House
House of the Duke of Beaufort.
Built around the end of the seventeenth century in Palladian style.
Fine collections of paintings and
furniture. Stables and hunt
kennels also open

Horton Court
Norman hall with small museum.
Fine old manor house with loggia
in garden

Little Sodbury Manor
Fifteenth century manor with fine
great hall and associations with
William Tyndale

Nan Tow's Tump
Best Cotswold round barrow

Sodbury Hillfort
Excellent site with recognisable
ditches and ramparts

Somerset Monument
Climbable tower with fine views
from the top

Below Hawkesbury is **Horton**, a
divided village; its church and court are
nearly ½ mile from the cottages and post
office. The court is interesting as part of
it is an unfortified Norman hall, (one of
the very few known) dating from around
1150, though the roof is at least 200
years later. The hall contains a small
museum of unrelated items — including
pewter and armour. The Court itself was
constructed around 1520 for Dr Knight,
a chief secretary to Henry VIII, who
negotiated with the Pope for the King's
divorce from Catherine of Aragon. The
Roman influence on Dr Knight can be
seen in the loggia in the gardens which
has the heads of some Roman emperors.

Next along the escarpment is **Little
Sodbury**, a tiny hamlet steeped in
English religious history. The tiny
church is dedicated to St Adeline, the
only church in England with that
dedication. The name may derive from a
convent near the Normandy home of the
first Norman lord, which was founded
by St Adeline. Perhaps the dedication is
another link with the imported Flemish
weavers, however, as Adeline was their
patron saint. The church originally
stood next to the manor house, but was
moved stone by stone to its present site
when it fell into disrepair. William

Acton Turville ▷

The Topps Memorial, Tormarton Church ▽

Tyndale must have preached regularly in the original church but little remains of it now. The pulpit has panels commemorating Tyndale and other, contemporary, martyrs.

 Up the hill from the church is Little Sodbury Manor. It is normally not open to the public but can be visited by appointment. The manor had a major restoration earlier this century, but retains the original fifteenth-century Great Hall, one of the finest known. King Henry VIII and Anne Boleyn spent a night here as guests of Sir John Walsh, the king's champion at his coronation. It was Sir John who employed a locally-born chaplain and tutor, William Tyndale, in 1521. Tyndale stayed for two years, moving abroad when his desire to have an English Bible embarrassed Sir John. Tyndale was executed for heresy in 1536, only two years before Henry VIII decreed that every English church should have an English Bible.

On the hill above the manor is the very fine Sodbury hillfort. It is not as large as Uleybury, but it is clearer. The ditches and ramparts are still deep and high, despite the erosion and infilling. Some idea of the massive undertaking can be gained by a walk around the ramparts. Its Iron Age builders constructed its defences so well that it continued to be used long after they had gone. There is evidence that the fort was occupied in Roman and Saxon times, and even as late as the fifteenth century by the army of Edward IV before the battle of Tewkesbury.

Little Sodbury is the smallest of the three Sodbury villages. **Old Sodbury**, the next village along the edge, is the

original. **Chipping Sodbury**, the newer market town, has a wide, airy main street.

South of Old Sodbury is Dodington Park, quite beautiful, a masterpiece of landscape gardening by Capability Brown. He not only planted trees in 'natural' positions, but also dug lakes, made valleys and built hills — an astonishing achievement. Several nature trails are signposted through the parkland, enabling one to explore the landscaping and the natural beauty. The house itself, built for the Codrington family in the eighteenth century, is massively constructed, with an elaborate columned entrance, but the more

delicate interior contains many fine pieces of work. It is not however open to the public.

Dodington village has little of great interest, but in the church is a memorial tablet to a member of the Codrington family, Sir Edward, who was captain of the Orion at the Battle of Trafalgar, and commander of the allied fleet at the Battle of Navarino. On the scarp top above Dodington is **Tormarton**, a small grey village with a church that has a memorial to Edward Topp, lord of the manor in the late seventeenth century. It is a relief sculpture of a mailed fist clutching a severed arm, all in full, gory colour.

To the east of Tormarton, the village of **Great Badminton** lies beside one of the most famous estates in Britain, the Beaufort. The name Badminton is famous throughout the world in two sports, the game named from the estate, and the three-day event, one of the world's foremost horse trials. The house is seventeenth century and a very fine example of this period. The interior is rich in decoration, some of it unique. The house stands in over 15,000 acres of parkland — the total estate being nearly 10 miles around. The park is partly natural, partly the work of Capability Brown, and partly formal. One of the more formal aspects, the Great Avenue, running down from Worcester Lodge and the A433 near Didmarton, is several miles long, and contains thousands of trees. Within the park are deer herds and several excellent follies.

The church at Great Badminton, next to the house, has a number of monuments to the Beaufort family. One to the first Duke, by Grinling Gibbons, is 25ft high, so big that the church had to be enlarged to accommodate it.

A little way south of Badminton, at **Acton Turville**, is beauty of a much simpler form and no less striking for that. The village contains little that is architecturally unique, but the old well, and its portcullis, are delightful.

East from Acton Turville the AONB points towards Wiltshire, as far as **Grittleton**. It has a manor house, described as a hideous monstrosity, the work of a committee, two architects and the owner, who seem to have spent most of the time at each others' throats.

Between Acton Turville and Grittleton is an excellent walk along the Foss Way. To reach the Way itself go along the lane towards Grittleton to Foss Gate, near the M4 motorway. Now follow the Way north, using bridle-paths for 1 or 1½ miles to return to the village.

W
4½m
1½h
oo
*

8 The Southwolds Around Bath

Having crossed into Wiltshire at the end of the previous chapter, we shall stay in that county moving south of the M4 motorway, to visit the villages of the By Brook valley. The brook rises near **Burton**, a small, neat village with a Georgian rectory, that actually stands on the border between Wiltshire and Gloucestershire. The church tower is one of the best in Wiltshire. Indeed there is a group of five churches with distinctive towers, considered not only to be extremely fine but to form a 'Wiltshire group', because they are sufficiently different from anything else of their architectural period (the Perpendicular). The AONB includes three of these churches, at Burton (although as a parish church this is shared by the village of Nettleton to the south), at West Kington, (a little way south of Nettleton) and at Yatton Keynell, to the west of Castle Combe.

Nettleton, a scattered hamlet close to

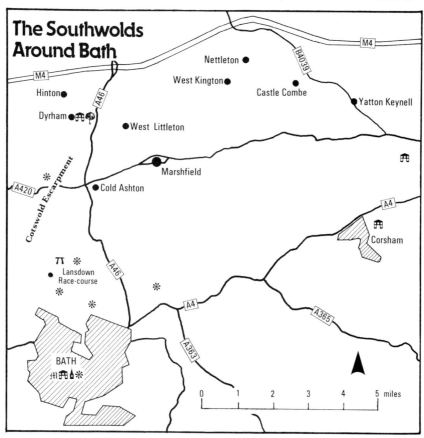

The Southwolds Around Bath

Nettleton ●

West Kington ●

Hinton ●

Dyrham ●

● West Littleton

● Marshfield

● Cold Ashton

Castle Combe ●

● Yatton Keynell

● Lansdown Race-course

Cotswold Escarpment

BATH

Corsham

0   1   2   3   4   5 miles

M4

B4039

A46

A420

A46

A4

A4

A365

A363

the Foss Way, has within its boundaries a collapsed long barrow with the loneliness that characterises these tombs, and the site of a Roman temple constructed among cliffs beside a stream flowing down to the By Brook. Both sites are visited by a walk that links Nettleton and West Kington by path or lane and then continues by lane and path past the temple site to the Foss Way. The Way, now a lane, is followed past Foss Farm to the woodland above By Brook. Here one goes left on a track to the Lugbury barrow. A wind-swept walk crosses the wold to a lane for Nettleton.

West Kington lies on the same stream that passes the temple site, Broadmead Brook, which rises closer to the A46. Its church is set on a hill, its tower thus set off to perfection. Inside is a pulpit that was used by Hugh Latimer while he was rector here, before becoming Bishop of Worcester. Latimer was executed by burning with Nicholas Ridley, Bishop of London, at Oxford, when they refused

to accept Catholicism after the accession of Queen Mary Tudor. Panels to these two martyrs are among those at Little Sodbury.

Further down the By Brook is the most famous of the valley villages, **Castle Combe**, one of the most picturesque in the entire Cotswolds. It is set in the valley, sheltered and secluded, almost part of a different world. On several occasions it has been used as a film location for period dramas.

The wealth of the village was based on sheep, as everywhere in the region, but Castle Combe had a charter to hold a fair, where sheep and wool changed hands, as well as other market goods. It was 'the most celebrated faire in North Wiltshire for sheep. . . whither sheep-masters doe come as far as from Northamptonshire'. To the north of the village there are the remains of the Norman castle built by one of the early lords of the manor. A memorial to this Lord, Walter de Dunstanville, is in the

W
4½m
1½h
oo
**

Castle Combe

The Royal Crescent, Bath

Bath Abbey

Castle Combe

church, a fine tomb with an effigy of the knight in a full suit of chain mail. The rest of the church is good, though extensive late nineteenth century restoration was not entirely satisfactory. For such a wealthy village, the church is not automatically recognisable as a wool church, although the tower, erected by local clothiers, is more elaborate than might be expected. The market cross stands at the village centre, covered by a roof on four pillars. To the west the restored Manor House, now a hotel, dates originally from the seventeenth century, as does Dower House to the north.

To the east of Castle Combe is **Yatton Keynell**, another of the group of five distinctive church towers. Keynell was added to the village's name by the lords of the manor who had the name. One of the earliest members of the family, Sir William, built the original church on this site: it was first dedicated to St Margaret of Antioch as a gesture of thanks for his safe return from the Crusades.

South of Yatton Keynell is a final piece of wold and at its centre is **Biddestone**, the old village in which is a final reminder of the grey Cotswold stone in true Cotswold landscape. Two miles east of Biddestone is Sheldon Manor; 2 miles to the south is Corsham Court. Sheldon Manor, one of the oldest houses in Wiltshire, dating in part from the thirteenth century, has been continuously lived in for nearly 700 years. In addition to the house itself, the visitor can wander among the terraced gardens. Corsham Court is Elizabethan and houses the Bath Academy of Art: its fine collection of paintings is based on the Methuen collection. The gardens are another example of the work of Brown and Repton.

Returning to Castle Combe, the By Brook can be followed southwards to the point where it leaves the AONB at **Slaughterford**, probably given that name, as with the Slaughters to the north, to distinguish the ford near the sloes from the other ford, to the north. The village has a mill, not for cloth or grain, but a paper mill.

The Almeshouses, Marshfield

South of Slaughterford the AONB turns north, avoiding the RAF station at Colerne, to meet the Foss Way at the

---

PLACES OF INTEREST AROUND
CORSHAM AND MARSHFIELD

Corsham Court
Elizabethan house with Georgian additions. Fine collections of paintings. Gardens by Brown and Repton

Dyrham Park
Fine house set in deer park

Sheldon Manor
Superb Plantagenet Manor with some thirteenth century work. Good terraced gardens with collections of old varieties of roses

Three-Shire Stone, nr Batheaston
Ancient boundary stone

---

pleasant Wraxall villages, North and Upper, set high above the By Brook. To the west, the traveller re-enters what was Gloucestershire but is now Avon, near the village of **Marshfield**. The tower of the church, visible for miles around, is the dominant feature within the village, standing at the 'Little' end. Near to it, Tolzey Hall, according to its inscription, was '. . . built by John Goslett, 1690. Was removed and rebuilt in 1793'.

At the far end of the delightful High Street are the almshouses built in the early seventeenth century for eight village old folk. Between the church and almshouses are a number of very fine inns.

North-west of Marshfield is the village of **Dyrham**, of picture-post-card beauty, containing several interesting sites. To the north of the village is Hinton Hill, on which can still be seen the remains of the medieval field system known as strip lynchets. This method of terracing sloping ground eased the labour of working such land, and in addition assisted crop rotation and the division of land. The hill is also the site of one of the most decisive battles during the invasion of Britain by the Anglo-Saxons, and the ousting of the British into Wales in favour of the English. The *Anglo-Saxon Chronicle* says that in 577 the Saxon kings Cuthwine and Ceawlin fought the Britons at Dyrham, killing three kings and capturing Gloucester, Cirencester and Bath. This simple, single-sentence entry conceals an event as significant as any in the history of Britain. The Saxons had been pushing westward across Britain for over a century, but their slow invasion had been halted, probably in Berkshire, by King Arthur at the battle of Badon around AD 500. With the death of Arthur, the Saxons advanced again. They cut the road from Gloucester and Cirencester to Bath, and encamped in the old hillfort at the summit of Hinton Hill. The three towns sent their armies to the site, where they attacked the well-defended Saxon army and were annihilated on the slopes of the hill. Following the battle, the British retreated to Wales and Cornwall, leaving what is now England to the

English. No memorial to the battle marks the hill, but it is as significant a battlefield as any in the country.

Dyrham church contains a memorial brass considered to be of similar age to the Berkeley brass at Wotton-under-Edge, and even possibly by the same artist. This one is to Sir Maurice Russell and his wife. The Latin inscription starts

Entombed here, bereft of life
Behold a gentle knight!

which is very poetic, even if a little has been lost in the translation. Immediately behind the church is Dyrham Park, a fine house and gardens, now in the hands of the National Trust. The original Tudor house was almost totally rebuilt about the end of the seventeenth century by William Blathwayt a Secretary of State to William III. The house is almost completely open to the public and, in addition to its architectural and decorative interest, there are fine collections of paintings, particularly by contemporary Dutch artists, and china. There is also a large greenhouse, one of the earliest known

Dyrham Park

115

examples. The park was laid out originally to include an extremely elaborate and very large water garden. Now, sadly, only the statue of Neptune in his fountain remains. The fountain has been dry for perhaps 200 years; the water garden fell into disrepair after only a relatively short time. The park, then landscaped by Repton, now contains a herd of the unusual fallow deer.

W
3m
1h
ooo
*

A good walk that encompasses Hinton Hill, Dyrham Park and village can be made by following the Cotswold Way from the village to the hill. Where it joins the lane, one goes down to the A46 and follows this with care to the park itself. One can return to the village by an exit at the lower end of the park.

To the south of Dyrham are **Doynton** — a pleasant village on the gentler bottom slopes of the escarpment, overlooking the outskirts of Bristol — and **Cold Ashton.** The latter is a quiet place with a church that was actually built by the rector, Thomas Key, in the early sixteenth century. The rector's mark, a T and a key interwined, can be seen in several places. The real mystery is where a humble country rector obtained enough money to build a church. But it is not the only mystery in Cold Ashton. One afternoon in the late 1930s a portrait painter, Olive Snell, set out to visit a friend in the Mendips: losing her way in the dark, she stopped at a house in Cold Ashton to ask the way and was directed by a man whom she tipped half a crown, assuming he was the butler. Her Mendip host could not understand the story as the house she described was empty and boarded up; so the ladies returned to Cold Ashton. The house was found, and it was indeed locked and chained: on the front door-step was the half-crown.

The exact house of this true story is not known. But there are a number of houses old enough and grand enough to have ghosts, none more so than Cold Ashton Manor, a fine building from 1600 to which Sir Bevil Granville was

brought. The word 'cold' was attached to the name to distinguish this village from another Ashton near Bristol. Probably 'Cold' was used because it best describes the village in the winter, for, situated at the head of St Catherine's valley, it can be a bleak place. But it has a fine view down the valley.

The valley itself is reminiscent of the wooded bottoms around Wotton-under-Edge. Here the sides are lower and shallower, and not as wooded, but it is still a fine valley. St Catherine's church dates, in part, from the thirteenth century, while the court, next door, is a much modified late fifteenth-century Benedictine monastery. The court was sold very cheaply by Henry VIII to his tailor John Malte, an act of generosity — unusual for Henry — prompted by

Hill, on its way from Bath to Wick. It is a massive structure, hardly elegant, but certainly imposing. Sir Bevil was a Cornishman, deeply committed to the Royalist cause in the Civil War, who brought a small army of men from Cornwall to assist the king. In 1643 these men joined a large Royalist Army at nearby Chewton Mendip and marched on Bath, then held for Parliament by Sir William Waller. Waller was a clever soldier and he took up a position not in the town, but at this tip of Lansdown Hill. The Royalist advance was halted by his cannon fire and the day seemed lost until Sir Bevil led his Cornishmen in a desperate attack up the slope. In truly heroic fashion, Sir Bevil rode up and across the hill, shouting encouragement, and the cannons were taken. But at the very moment of victory, Sir Bevil was unseated and wounded: he was taken to Cold Ashton Manor, where he died that night. The battle for Bath continued, and when it was eventually taken, the Cornishmen had the honour of being the first troops to enter the city. The memorial was erected by a grandson who was ennobled and took the title Lansdown.

Malte's adoption and removal from the Royal Court of an illegitimate daughter of the king. The walk from below, back along the east side of the river is waymarked through meadowland, and affords fine views of the court itself.

The valley represents the southern tip of the Cotswolds, the AONB boundary being near Batheaston. To the west the Area extends southwards to its western extremity at **Upton Cheney**, a village with a splendid name, on the side of another Golden Valley, with the River Boyd flowing down one side of Bristol to reach the Avon. The Area just includes Hanging Hill, a bleakly-named hill from the top of which there are views across Lansdown and to the Bevil Grenville memorial. This stands near the top of the minor road that crosses Lansdown

An interesting walk from the racecourse (on Lansdown Hill) is to skirt it on its northern side, from the minor road or golfcourse, joining the Cotswold Way on the escarpment edge near the starting gates. From here it is a short walk to Prospect Stile, from which there are fine views to the Avon Valley and to Kelston Round Hill, a distinctive mound to the south, topped by a copse of trees. A return can be made on the southern side of the racecourse.

Though **Bath** does not actually lie within the Cotswolds it is impossible not to regard it as a Cotswold town, the Bath stone of the buildings being from the same bedrock as the villages of the northern towns. Its origins are steeped in mystery. It is likely that earliest man

W
4m
1¼h
oo
*

Pulteney Bridge, Bath

knew of the existence of the hot springs, although as the surrounding area is likely to have been a salt marsh, he may not have had a home here. According to legend the town was built by Prince Bladud, descendent of refugees from Troy, and father of Shakespeare's King Lear. The poor prince contracted leprosy and was immediately banished from court to live out his days as a pig herder in the marshes. Inevitably one of the pigs also contracted leprosy but to Bladud's astonishment it was cured after taking a mud-bath near the hot springs. Bladud then tried the mud-bath himself and he, too, was cured, and allowed back to court. To commemorate this legendary founding of the city, about 2,800 years ago, there are statues to Bladud at the baths.

The archaeological evidence of the founding of the city is more mundane. It is likely that the first town was Roman, *Aquæ Sulis* — the waters of the goddess Sulis — constructed in the first century AD. The Romans were undoubtedly tempted by the 250,000 gallons of water at 120^{0}F that rushed to the surface daily, and constructed a town around the public baths. The baths themselves are a minor wonder, with central heating in all rooms, a sauna and, of course, the pool, all fed by the hot waters. When the Romans left, the town quickly decayed. The Saxon invaders, reaching here after the battle of Dyrham, could only wonder at the building. They were not great builders themselves and they believed the town was the work of giants, and haunted. Certainly the decaying buildings, the deep, warm pools, all overgrown, must have been ghostly. Gradually the site became holy, probably fired by superstition and legend, and King Offa founded an abbey here. This became an important site, and King Edgar was crowned here in 973. The abbot and the townspeople of medieval Bath knew of the hot waters and their medicinal purposes, for there are early references to the town to bathe in the waters. Indeed the visitors were a

American Museum, Bath
Domestic life in seventeenth to nineteenth century America. Wild West and Indian collections

Beckford Tower, Bath
Fine views from the top

Bookbinding Museum, Bath
Attached to bookshop. History of the craft

Camden Works, Bath
Museum of industrial Bath with a complete Victorian brass foundry

Carriage Museum, Bath
Museum of the finest collection of horse-drawn carriages in Britain. Daily rides in summer.

Costume Museum, Bath
Based on the collection of Doris Langley Moore. Fashion from Shakespearean times. Collections of jewellery and dolls

Exhibition Rooms, Bath
Contains the Charles Moore geological collection, as well as other exhibitions

Herschel House, Bath
Small museum of Herschel's work in music and astronomy in his Bath house

Victoria Art Gallery, Bath
Collections of European, eighteenth to twentieth century British work and that of local artists. Also collections of porcelain, glass and early watches.

Guildhall, Bath
Fine eighteenth-century building with excellent banqueting hall.

Holburne of Menstrie Museum, Bath
Excellent collections of silver, porcelain, furniture and paintings in fine eighteenth century mansion. Licensed teahouse from May to September.

Postal Museum, Bath
Next to the Victorian pillar box. New museum that will cover all aspects of the postal service, but particularly the mailcoach era

Roman Baths, Bath
Exhibition of the Roman town of *Aquæ Sulis* excavated on this and other city sites. The ruins of the baths themselves can be visited

No 1 Royal Crescent
Recreation of a Georgian house in the most famous of Bath's buildings

Royal Photographic Society's National Centre of Photography
Exhibitions of historic and contemporary photographs

Toy Museum, Bath
Devoted to toys, dolls and games from the early nineteenth century to the present

Underground Ammunition Depot
World's largest underground depot, now empty, carved from solid rock

Claverton Pumping Station
Pumphouse including a 24ft waterwheel.

Bath Abbey

major source of income to the towns-people.

The bathers were subject to no regulations, however, and the baths were so unwholesome that people were reluctant to use them. It was noted in 1533 that the chief bathers were those with 'lepre, pokkes, scabbes and great aches' and since there was no filtration or effective changing of the water it is hardly surprising that the baths were described as stinking. As with Cheltenham, Bath had to wait 200 years for the coming of a gentler age. Unlike Cheltenham, Bath had Richard (Beau) Nash. It was he who regulated the bathing, stopped the sedan chair carriers from overcharging, erected theatres, assembly rooms and houses, and controlled the gambling that was at the heart of Bath's social position. The whole Georgian city is really a tribute to the energy of this one man, who died in 1761 at the great age of 88. His statue

stands in the Pump Room, which dispenses warm salty water freely to visitors.

Architecturally and historically, Bath requires a guide book of its own. To see some, and by no means all, of the better buildings, the visitor can take a short walk from the abbey. Across Orange Grove is the River Avon, crossed a little way north by Pulteney Bridge, a fine Georgian structure, near the City Library and Art Gallery. Orange Grove is named after the Prince of Orange and at its centre is an obelisk raised by Beau Nash to commemorate the Prince's visit to the city. South of the abbey is North Parade Passage, or Old Lilliput Alley where there are Bath's oldest houses, built around 1500.

The abbey itself is a masterpiece; it was started about 1500 on the site of an older, Norman, church. Its construction followed a dream by Oliver King, Bishop of Bath and Wells, in which he

T
2m
oo
*

The Circus, Bath

saw angels climbing ladders to heaven and was told to rebuild the older church. The abbey's west front follows King's dream with angels actually climbing ladders on either side. The architects employed by King promised him that 'ther shal be noone so goodly in england nor in fraunce'. And who would argue with the truth of that promise? A statue of Bishop King can be seen inside. Other important memorials are to Beau Nash and Sir William Waller's wife. Prior Birde's notable chantry is on the south side of the chancel. The stonework here is magnificent; indeed so fine is it that the time spent by the masons on its construction bankrupted the benefactor.

Leaving the abbey churchyard to the west the visitor reaches the Pump Room (built at the latter end of the eighteenth century) and the Roman Baths. Westward again are two of the original baths, the Cross Bath in Bath Street and the Hot Bath. Travelling north the visitor can see the Theatre Royal, part of which was once Beau Nash's house, and, beyond, Queen Square, considered to be one of the best works in the city by John Wood the Elder, who with his son, John the Younger, formed the principal team of architects of the Georgian city that lies to the north of the baths. The obelisk is, again, a commemoration by Beau Nash, this time of Frederick, Prince of Wales. Running north from the Square is Gay Street built by the Woods; Josiah Wedgwood, the famous pottery manufacturer, lived here at No 30.

At the top of Gay Street is the Circus, a magnificent circular building by the Woods. Here lived, though not at the same time, William Pitt, Gainsborough and David Livingstone. To the east are the Assembly Rooms by Wood the Younger. West from the Circus is Brock Street, leading to Royal Crescent, perhaps the best known and loved of all Bath's buildings. The Crescent is by John Wood the Younger, and is superbly set off by the lawns and trees in

The Assembly Rooms, Bath

front of it. Sir Isaac Pitman lived here and from here Sheridan eloped with Elizabeth Linley. William Herschel, an organist, lived in nearby New King Street: he made telescopes as a hobby and used one to discover the planet Uranus, later becoming Astronomer Royal. His house in New King Street — Herschel House, at No 19 — is now a museum of his music and astronomy. It is one of Bath's many museums.

No 1 Royal Crescent is another museum, owned by the Bath Preservation Trust, and has been completely restored to its eighteenth century state. At the Assembly Rooms is the Museum of Costume, one of the world's largest displays, covering fashion back to medieval times, and including exhibitions of jewellery. No 4 The Circus is an extension of the museum that holds the library of books, magazines and photographs of fashion.

Behind the Circus, in Circus Mews, is the Carriage Museum, a collection of thirty carriages, some of which are used occasionally, and one of which has been used at Coronations. In addition there is a collection of livery equipment from the 'Great Age of Coaching', of which the Cotswolds in general, and Bath in particular, saw a great deal. The museum offers rides daily in summer. In Manvers Street a book-selling and binding shop has been extended to produce the Museum of Bookbinding where the history and considerable art of the craft are explained and displayed. The Toy Museum in York Street has dolls and dolls' houses, great games and many other toys from past years.

A fascinating addition to Bath's museums is the Postal Museum at 8 Broad Street. The city has very strong links with the postal service, and is grateful to it. Ralph Allen, a Cornishman, rented the postal service from the Government in the late seventeenth century and made it efficient and profitable. In the process he became rich, and his arrival in Bath, around 1710, was the start of Bath's rise to fame. It was Allen who saw the potential of the hot springs and bought the Combe

Down quarries that supplied the stone for his architect, John Wood the Elder, who designed Allen's own house, near the abbey. All aspects of the postal service and the Royal Mail are covered.

The Royal Photograhpic Society has its National Centre for Photography in The Octagon, Milsom Street. It has both an exhibition centre and a museum of photography. In Sydney Place, at the far end of the Great Pulteney Street, is the Holburne of Menstrie Museum, part of the University of Bath. This contains the collections of Sir Thomas Holburne: paintings, including works by Gainsborough, Stubbs and Reynolds; silver, one of the finest collections in Britain; porcelain and glass; bronzes and enamels. In addition to the set collections, there are special exhibitions during the year, and a Craft Study Centre for modern craftwork in metal and glass. Outside, the gardens are also of interest.

At the other end of the street, beyond Pulteney Bridge, the Victoria Art Gallery houses, in addition to paintings, fine collections of glass and ceramics, and items of local interest. Many times during the year there are special exhibitions covering a range of subjects. The Roman Museum at the Pump Room houses many of the items found during excavations on the site and elsewhere in the city. Particularly noticeable are the head of Medusa, a stone carving from the Roman Temple, and a bronze head of Minerva.

Finally within the city, there are the Exhibition rooms at 18 Queen Square. Here is housed the geological collection of Charles Moore, concerned chiefly with local geology. Other rooms have special exhibitions that are changed at regular intervals. Away from the city centre there are three further museums. The Museum of Bath at Work is at the Camden Works, Julian Street, to the north of the Assembly Rooms: here the visitor can get away from the social elegance of Georgian Bath to discover how the ordinary city dweller lived in the eighteenth ad nineteenth centuries. The Works themselves are an exact reconstruction of a Victorian brass foundry, with other exhibits illustrating different industries and lifestyles.

The American Museum at Claverton Manor, two miles east of the city centre, shows the history of North America from the time of the Pilgrim Fathers: exhibits deal with the opening of the West and with the Indians, and in the gardens there is a teepee and a covered wagon. From Beckford Tower, near Lansdown — it contains a museum to William Beckford — there are some outstanding views.

Further Information___

The information given below has been obtained from a number of sources. Admission charges have not been included as they are subject to revision.

The details are correct at the time of publication, but are also subject to revision and should be checked beforehand if there is any doubt. This is particularly true for opening times at Bank Holidays. Most of the sites listed below close at Christmas and New Year, but are open at Easter and all other Bank Holidays. This is not true of all sites, and there are changes from year to year.

RECOMMENDED WALKS

Town Walks
1 Chipping Campden
2 Painswick
3 Bath

Wold and Valley Walks
1 Dover's Hill to Kiftsgate Stone (Chapter 1)
2 Laverton to Stanton, the spring line villages (Chapter 1)
3 Slaughterbrook (Chapter 2)
4 Barrington Valley (Chapter 4)
5 Chedworth Wood (Chapter 5)
6 Haresfield Beacon (Chapter 6)

BUILDINGS AND GARDENS OPEN TO THE PUBLIC

Ampney Park Gardens
Ampney Crucis
Tel: Poulton 534
Open: April to September, Tuesday and Saturday 2–6pm. At other times by prior appointment.

Badminton House
Badminton
Tel: Badminton 202
Open: specific dates only, check locally for details.

Barnsley House Gardens
Barnsley, Cirencester
Tel: Bibury 281
Open: all year, Wednesday, 10am-6pm; first Sunday in May, June and July, 2–7pm.

Berkeley Castle
Berkeley
Tel: Dursley 810332
Open: April to September, daily (except Monday) 2–5pm; May to August, weekdays (except Monday), 11am–5pm, Sunday 2-5pm; October, Sunday, 2–4.30pm Bank Holidays 11am–5pm.

Bredon Springs
Ashton-under-Hill
Tel: Evesham 881328
Open; April to October, Wednesday, Thursday, Saturday and Sunday, 10am–dusk, Bank Holidays and Tuesday 10am—dusk.

Buckland Rectory
Buckland
Tel: Broadway 2479
Open: May to July and September, Monday 11am–4pm; August, Monday and Friday, 11am–4pm.

Chavenage House
Tetbury
Tel: Tetbury 52329
Open: May to September, Thursday, Sunday and Bank Holidays, 2–5pm.

Chastleton House
Moreton-in-Marsh
Tel: Barton-on-the-Heath 355
Open: Easter to September, Friday,
Saturday, Sunday and Bank Holidays,
2–5pm.

Cheltenham College
Bath Road, Cheltenham
Tel: Cheltenham 43094
Open: any reasonable time, by
arrangement with the bursar's office.

Corsham Court
Corsham
Tel: Corsham 712214
Open: mid-January to mid-December,
daily (except Monday and Friday)
2–4pm; June to September, daily (except
Monday and Friday) and Bank Holidays
2–6pm.

Daneway House
Sapperton
Tel: Frampton Mansell 232
Open: March to October, by
appointment only.

Dyrham Park (NT)
Dyrham
Tel: Abson 2501
Open: *House and Park,* April, May and
October, daily (except Thursday and
Friday) 2–6pm or dusk if earlier; June to
September daily (except Friday) 2-6pm.
Park only, all year, daily 12noon–6pm

Ernest Wilson Memorial Gardens
Chipping Campden
Open: all year at reasonable times.

Hidcote Manor Gardens (NT)
Hidcote Bartrim
Tel: Mickleton 333
Open: April to October, daily (except
Tuesday and Friday) 11am–8pm.

Horton Court (NT)
Horton
Open: April to October, Wednesday and
Saturday 2–6pm or sunset; other times
by written appointment only.

Kiftsgate Court Gardens
Nr Chipping Campden
Open: April to September, Wednesday,
Thursday and Sunday 2–6pm.

Little Sodbury Manor
Little Sodbury
Tel: Chipping Sodbury 312232
Open: April to September, by
appointment only.

Minchinhampton Market House
Market House, Minchinhampton
Tel: Dursley 883241
Open: all year, Saturday, Sunday and
Bank Holidays 9am–5.30pm; other
times by appointment only.

Miserden Park
Nr. Stroud
Tel: Miserden 303
Open: all year, Wednesday and
Thursday, 10am–4.30pm.

Newark Park (NT)
Ozleworth
Tel: Dursley 842644
Open: April, May, August and
September, Wednesday and Thursday
2–5pm; other times by appointment
only.

Owlpen Manor
Owlpen, nr Uley
Open: June and July, Friday 2–6pm.

Painswick House
Painswick
Tel: Painswick 813646
Open: July to September, Saturday,
Sunday and Bank Holidays 2-6pm

Pittville Pump Room
Albert Road, Cheltenham
Tel: Cheltenham 21621
Open: May to October, Tuesday-Sunday
10am–5pm; November to March,
Tuesday-Saturday 10.30am–5pm.

The Priory
Kemerton
Tel: Overbury 258
Open:June to September, Thursday and
certain Sundays 2-7pm

Sezincote Gardens
Sezincote, nr Moreton-in-Marsh
Tel: Blockley 70444
Open: all year (except December),
Thursday and Friday 2–4pm; Bank
Holidays 2–4pm.
House Open May, June, July and
September, Thursday and Friday
2.30–5.30pm.

Sheldon Manor
Nr Chippenham
Tel: Chippenham 653120
Open: April to September, Thursday,
Sunday and Bank Holidays, 12.30–6pm.

Snowshill Manor
Snowshill
Tel: Broadway 852410
Open: May to September, Wednesday-
Sunday and Bank Holiday Monday
11am–1pm, 2–6pm or sunset; April and
October, Saturday, Sunday and Bank
Holidays 11am–1pm, 2-6pm

Stanway House
Stanway
Tel: Stanway 469
Open: June, July and August, Tuesday
and Thursday 2–5pm.

Sudeley Castle
Winchcombe
Tel: Winchcombe 602308
Open: *Grounds*, April to October, daily
11am–5.30pm.
Castle, April to October, daily
12noon–5pm.

Upper Slaughter Manor
Upper Slaughter
Tel: Bourton-on-the-Water 20927
Open: May to September, Friday
2–5.30pm

Westonbirt House
Westonbirt School, nr Tetbury
Tel: Westonbirt 333
Open: Check with local Tourist
Information Office for details.

MUSEUMS AND ART GALLERIES   ℳ

American Museum
Claverton Manor, Bath
Tel: Bath 60503
Open: April to October, daily (except
Monday) 2—5pm, Bank Holiday Sunday
and Monday, 11am–5pm.

Arlington Mill Museum
Bibury
Tel: Bibury 368
Open: March to October, daily
10.30am–7pm; November to February,
Saturday and Sunday 10.30am–7pm.

Beatrix Potter Museum
Tailor of Gloucester's House
9 College Court, Gloucester
Tel: Gloucester 422856
Open: all year, Monday-Saturday
9.30am–5pm.

Beckford Tower
Lansdown, Bath
Tel: Bath 858106
Open: April to October, Saturday,
Sunday, and Bank Holidays 2–5pm

Bookbinding Museum
Manvers Street, Bath
Tel: Bath 66000
Open: April to September, Monday-
Friday 9.30am–5.30pm; other times by
appointment only

Camden Works
Julian Road, Bath
Tel: Bath 318348
Open: all year, daily (except Friday),
2-5pm; Easter-October, daily 2-5pm.

Carriage Museum
Circus Mews, Bath
Tel: Bath 25175
Open: all year, daily 10am–5.30pm.

Cider Mill Gallery
Blanchworth Farm, nr Stinchcombe
Tel: Dursley 2352
Open: June to August, Tuesday-Sunday
11am–5pm: April, May, September and
December, Tuesday-Saturday 11am–
5pm.

Cirencester Lock-Up
Trinity Road, Cirencester
Open: April to September, Monday-
Saturday 10am–5.30pm, Sunday
2–5.30pm; October to March, Tuesday-
Saturday. The Lock-Up is administered
by the Corinium Museum.

City Museum and Art Gallery
Brunswick Road, Gloucester
Tel: Gloucester 24131
Open: all year, Monday-Saturday
10am–5pm, Sunday (August only)
2–5pm.

Claverton Pumping Station
Ferry Lane, Claverton, Bath
Tel: Bristol 712939
Open: April to October, Sunday
10am–5pm.
On some Sundays the machinery is
operated.

Corinium Museum
Park Street, Cirencester
Tel: Cirencester 5611
Open: April to September, Monday-
Saturday, 10am–5.30pm, Sunday,
2–5.30pm
October to March, Tuesday-Saturday
10am–5pm, Sunday 2–5pm

Costume Museum
Assembly Rooms, Bath
Tel: Bath 61111
Open: April to October, daily
9.30am–6pm,Sunday 10am–6pm;
November to March, daily 10am–5pm,
Sunday 11am–5pm.

Cotswold Countryside Collection
Northleach
Tel: Northleach 715 or Cirencester 5611
Open: April to October, Monday-
Saturday 10am–5.30pm.

Cross Tree Gallery
Filkins, Nr Lechlade
Open: June to September, Monday-
Saturday 10am–5.30pm; October to
May, Tuesday-Saturday 10am–5.30pm

Dowty Railway Society
Northway Lane, Ashchurch, nr
Tewkesbury
Tel: Tewkesbury 292441
Open: all year, Sunday 2–5pm.
Special steam days

Fashion Research Centre
4 The Circus, Bath
Open: all year, daily 10am–1pm, 2–5pm.

Folk Museum
Town Hall, Winchcombe
Tel: Winchcombe 602925
Open: May to October, daily,
10am–5pm.

Folk Museum (Bishop Hooper's
Lodgings)
99-103 Westgage Street, Gloucester
Tel: Gloucester 26467
Open: all year Monday-Saturday
10am–5pm.

Geology Museum
18 Queen Square, Bath
Tel: Bath 28144
Open: all year, Monday-Friday
10am–6pm, Sunday, 10am–5pm; Closed
Bank Holidays

Guildhall
High Street, Bath
Tel: Bath 61111
Open: all year, Monday-Thursday
8.30am–5pm, Friday 8.30am–4pm.

Gustav Holst Birthplace Museum
4 Clarence Road, Cheltenham
Tel: Cheltenham 524846
Open: all year, Tuesday-Friday
10am–5.30pm, Saturday, 11am–5.30pm;
closed Bank Holidays.

Herschel House
19 New King Street, Bath
Tel: Bath 336228
Open: March to October, Wednesday,
Saturday and Sunday 2–5pm.

Holburne of Menstrie Museum
Great Pulteney Street, Bath
Tel: Bath 66669
Open: all year, Monday to Saturday
11am–5pm, Sunday 2.30–6pm; closed
January and Mondays November to
Easter.

Jenner Museum
3 Church Lane, Berkeley
Tel: Dursley 810631
Open: April to September, Tuesday-
Sunday 2.30–6pm; Bank Holidays
2.30–6pm.

John Moore Museum
Church Street, Tewkesbury
Tel: Tewkesbury 297174
Open: Easter to October, Tuesday-
Saturday 10am–1pm, 2–5pm; Bank
Holidays 10am–1pm, 2–5pm; occasional
Sunday in summer 2–5pm.

Little Museum
45 Church Street, Tewkesbury
Tel: Tewkesbury 297114
Open: Easter to October, Tuesday-
Saturday 10am–5pm

Motor Museum
Bourton-on-the-Water
Tel: Bourton-on-the-Water 21255
Open: daily 10am–6pm.

Museum of Newspapers and Caricatures
39 Church Street, Tewkesbury
Tel: Tewkesbury 298484
Open: all year, Tuesday-Saturday
10am–1pm, 2–5pm; Bank Holidays
11am–5pm.

Pittville Pump Room Museum
Pittville Park, Cheltenham
Open: November to March, daily
(except Sunday and Monday)
10.30am–5pm; April to October, daily
(except Monday) 10.30am–5pm.

Police Bygones Museum
The Old Court House, Long Street,
Tetbury
Open: all year, Monday-Saturday
10am–4.30pm

Police Museum
Old Town Hall, Winchcombe
Open: all year, Monday-Saturday
10am–4.30pm

Postal Museum
8 Broad Street, Bath
Tel: Bath 60333
Open: all year, Monday to Saturday
11am–5pm, Sunday 2–6pm

Railway Museum
Winchcombe
Tel: Winchcombe 602257
Open: Easter and Bank Holidays,
Sunday and Monday 2.30–6pm; July,
Sunday 2.30–6pm; August, Monday-
Saturday 2–9pm, Sunday 2.30–6pm

Regimental Museum
The Old Customs House, Commercial
Road, Gloucester
Tel: Gloucester 22682
Open: all year, Monday-Friday
10am–5pm

Robert Opie Collection
Albert Warehouse, Gloucester Docks,
Gloucester
Tel: Gloucester 32309
Open: all year, Tuesday-Sunday
10am–6pm; Bank Holidays 10am–6pm.

Roman Baths Museum
Pump Room, Bath
Tel: Bath 61111
Open: April to October, daily 9am–6pm;
November to March, Monday to
Saturday 9am–5pm, Sunday 10am–5pm.

No 1 Royal Crescent
Bath
Tel: Bath 28126
Open: March to October, Tuesday-
Saturday 11am-5pm, Sunday 2-5pm

**Royal Photographic Society National
Centre of Photography**
The Octagon, Milsom Street, Bath
Tel: Bath 62841
Open: all year, Monday-Saturday
10am-5.30pm, Sunday (summer only)
10am-4.45pm in summer only

Smerril Farm Museum
Kemble, nr Cirencester
Tel: Kemble 208
Open: all year, daily 10.30am-6pm.

Swinford Museum
Filkins, nr Lechlade
Tel: Filkins 365
April to October, Thursday-Saturday
10am-6pm.

Tolsey Museum
High Street, Burford
Open: Easter to October, daily
2.30-5.30pm.

Town and District Museum
Lansdown, Stroud
Tel: Stroud 3394
Open: all year, Monday-Friday
10.30am-1pm, 2-5pm.

Town Museum
64 Barton Street, Tewkesbury
Tel: Tewkesbury 295027
Open: April to October, daily
10am-1pm, 2-5pm.

Town Museum and Art Gallery
Clarence Street, Cheltenham
Tel: Cheltenham 37431
Open: all year, Monday-Saturday
10am-5.30pm

Toy Museum
York Street, Bath
Tel: Bath 61819
Open: all year, daily 10am-5.30pm.

Transport Museum
Bearland, Gloucester
The museum is not open to the public
but is visible from the road at all times.

Underground Ammunition Depot
Monkton Farleigh, Nr Bath
Tel: Bath 852400
Open: Easter to October, daily
10am-6pm; November to Easter,
Saturday and Sunday 10am-6pm.

Victoria Art Gallery
Bridge Street, Bath
Tel: Bath 61111
Open: all year, Monday-Friday
10am-6pm, Saturday 10am-5pm.

Village Life Exhibition
The Old Mill, Bourton-on-the-Water
Tel: Bourton-on-the-Water 21255
Open: all year, daily 10am-6pm.

Woolstapler's Hall Museum
High Street, Chipping Campden
Tel: Evesham 840289
Open: April to September, daily
11am-6pm; October, Saturday and
Sunday 11am-6pm.

COUNTRY PARKS AND PICNIC SITES

Broadway Tower Country Park
Fish Hill, Broadway
Tel: Broadway 852390
Open: April to early October, daily
10am-5pm

Coaley Peak Picnic Site
Nr Frocester
Open: at all reasonable times.

Crickley Hill Country Park
Above Witcombe
Open: at all reasonable times.

Tog Hill Picnic Site
Nr Cold Ashton
Open at all reasonable times.

ARBORETA

Batsford Park
Batsford, Nr Bourton-on-the-Hill
Tel: Blockley 700409
Open: April to November, daily
10am–5pm.

Westonbirt (Forestry Commission)
Westonbirt, Nr Tetbury
Tel: Westonbirt 220
Open: all year, daily 10am–8pm or
sunset.

MAJOR ARCHAEOLOGICAL AND HISTORICAL SITES

All sites are open at any reasonable time,
unless stated otherwise

Arlington Row (NT)
Bibury
Not open to the public. Exterior only
may be viewed

Belas Knap Long Barrow (English
Heritage)
Nr Winchcombe

Blackfriars (English Heritage)
Gloucester
Open: April to September, Monday-
Saturday 9.30am–6.30pm, Sunday
2–6pm

Bredon Tithe Barn (NT)
Bredon
Open: all year, Wednesday and
Thursday 2–6pm, Saturday and Sunday
10am–6pm.

Chedworth Roman Villa (NT)
Yanworth
Tel: Withington 256
Open: March to October, Tuesday-
Sunday and Bank Holidays 11am–6pm;
November to mid-December and
February, Wednesday-Sunday
11am–4pm.

City East Gate
Eastgate Street, Gloucester
Open: May to September, Wednesday,
Friday and Saturday 2–5pm.

Crickley Hillfort
Crickley Hill Country Park

Frocester Tithe Barn
Frocester Court
Tel: Stonehouse 3250

Greyfriars
Gloucester

Hailes Abbey (English Heritage and NT)
Nr Oldbury-on-the-Hill
Tel: Winchcombe 602398
Open: April to September, daily
9.30am–6.30pm; late March, and early
October, Monday-Saturday,
9.30am–6.30pm, and Sunday 2–6.30pm.

Hetty Pegler's Tump (or Uley Tumulus)
(English Heritage)
Nr Uley
Key for door available from Crawley
Barns, ½ mile south

Kiftsgate Stone
Above Chipping Campden

Kingswood Abbey Gatehouse
Kingswood

Minster Lovell Hall (English Heritage)
Minster Lovell, Nr Burford
Tel: Asthall Leigh 315
Open: March, April and October,
Monday-Saturday 9.30am–5.30pm,
Sunday 2–5.30pm; May to September,
Monday-Saturday 9.30am–7pm, Sunday
2–7pm; November and February,
Monday-Friday 9.30am–4pm, Sunday
2–4pm.

Nan Tow's Tump
Nr Hawkesbury Upton

Notgrove Long Barrow
Notgrove

Nympsfield Long Barrow
Coaley Peak Picnic Site

Rollright Stones
Nr Long Compton

Roman Baths
Pump Room, Bath
Tel: Bath 61111
Open: April to October, daily 9am–
6pm; November to March, Monday–
Saturday 9am–5pm, Sunday 11am–5pm.

Sodbury Hillfort
Above Little Sodbury

Uleybury Hillfort
Above Uley

Uley Tumulus
See Hetty Pegler's Tump

Witcombe Roman Villa
Nr Great Witcombe
Key available from nearby farmhouse

Woodchester Roman Pavement
Replica at: Rowland Hill's Tabernacle
Church
Wotton-under-Edge
Open: all year, daily 10am–6pm

VIEWPOINTS AND SHORT WALKS

Barrow Wake
Geological Dial above Witcombe.

Cleeve Common
Nr Cheltenham
Highest point of Cotswolds. Panorama
Dial

Dover's Hill
Above Chipping Campden
Panorama Dial

Frocester Hill
Coaley Peak Picnic Site
Panorama Dial.

Haresfield Beacon
Above Haresfield
Topograph on nearby point (nr Standish
Wood).

Kilkenny Viewpoint
Nr Andoversford

Leckhampton Hill and Charlton Kings Common
Above Leckhampton

Penn Hill
Above Weston, nr Bath

Prospect Stile
Lansdown Racecourse, nr Bath

ANIMALS, BIRDS, ETC   ❼

Birdland Zoo Gardens and Birdland Art Gallery
Bourton-on-the-Water
Tel: Bourton-on-the-Water 20689/20480
Open: March to November, daily
10am–6pm; December to February,
daily 10.30am–4pm.

Bird Park
Prinknash Abbey Park
Tel: Painswick 812455
Open: Easter to October, daily
10am–6pm.

Butterfly Exhibition
High Street, Bourton-on-the-Water
Tel: Bourton-on-the-Water 20712
Open: all year, daily 11am–7pm.

Cotswold Farm Park
Bemborough Farm, Nr Guiting Power
Tel: Guiting Power 307
Open: May to September, daily
10.30am–6pm.

Cotswold Wildlife Park
Nr Burford
Tel: Burford 3006
Open: all year, daily 10am–6pm.

Folly Farm Waterfowl
Bourton-on-the-Water
Tel: Bourton-on-the-Water 20285
Open: all year, 1–6pm or dusk.

Trout Farm
Bibury
Tel: Bibury 215
Open: Mid-March to Christmas,
Monday-Friday 1–6pm, Saturday and
Sunday 11am–6pm.

Trout Farm
Condicote Lane, Donnington
Tel: Stow-on-the-Wold 30873
Open: November to March, daily
10am–5pm; April to October, daily
10am–6pm.

Trout Farm
Rissington Road, Bourton-on-the-Water
Tel: Bourton-on-the-Water 20541
Open: March to November, daily
10.30am–6pm.

Wildfowl Trust
Slimbridge
Tel: Cambridge (Glos) 333
Open: all year, daily 9.30am–5pm or
dusk.

 FARM TRAILS

Bemborough Farm Trail
Bemborough Farm, Nr Guiting Power
(same site as the Cotswold Farm Park)
Open: March to September, daily
10.30am–6pm.

Denfurlong Farm Trail
Denfurlong Farm, Nr Chedworth
Open: all year, daylight hours.

In addition to the above Warden Service
of the Cotswold AONB offers a number
of open days on farms throughout the
area during the summer months. Details
can be obtained from:

Gloucester County Council
Planning Department
Shire Hall, Gloucester
Tel: Gloucester 21444
A sae would be appreciated. Details of
the programme of open days are also
available in local libraries

CRAFT CENTRES

Because of the nature of the Cotswolds
almost all the larger villages, and a good
number of the smaller ones, have craft
shops. A large number also support
local craftsmen. It is impossible,
therefore, to be exhaustive, but
particular note should be made of the
following:

Chipping Campden
Guild of Handicrafts active at several
places in the town

Cirencester
The Workshops
Cricklade Street
Tel: Cirencester 61566
Open: all year, Monday-Saturday
10am–5.30pm.

Cotswold Woollen Weavers
Filkins, Nr Lechlade
Tel: Filkins 491
Open: all year, Monday-Saturday
10am–6pm, Sunday 2–6pm.

The Craftsman's Market
Corn Hall, Cirencester
Open: March to December, 1st and 3rd
Saturday in the month
Open for buying and commissioning
crafts. As many as 40 workers present

Painswick
August, Annual Exhibition of the Guild
of Gloucester Craftsmen

132

The Cotswold Village of
BLOCKLEY
GLOUCESTERSHIRE,
showing some of its notable buildings
including the historic water-mills
(all of which are now in private occupation)
Mills are numbered 1 to 12 on insets
and map, other buildings 13 to 22

Ebene

Milldene (corn, grist & iron foundry)

The Warren

Tombstone to a Trout at Fish Cottage

Rock Cottage
Home of Joanna Southcott

Malvern House

Russell Spring

DAYS LANE

HIGH

Woolstaplers Hall

Dovedale House

Penners Quarry

DONKEY LANE

Old Mill (flour)

① Dovedale Mill (flour and chaff)

② Malvern Mill (silk, cider, threshing)

③ Mill Close (silk, electricity & village institute)

㉑ Church Gates

B4479

MORETON-IN-MARSH

1973 revised 1984

(TO A44)

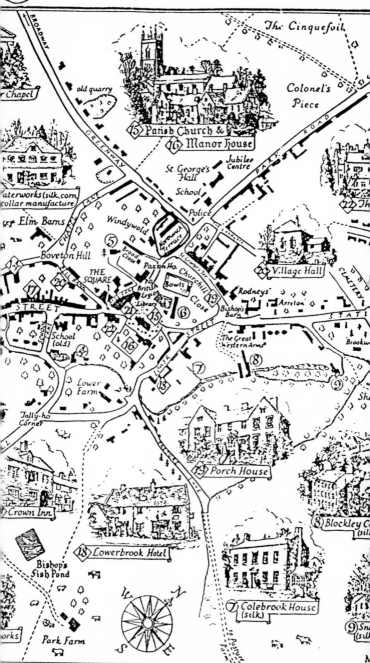

TO A44

BROADWAY

The Cinquefoil

Colonel's Piece

old quarry

r Chapel

GREENWAY

CHAPEL LANE

DAXEY ROAD

15 Parish Church & 16 Manor House

St. George's Hall

Jubilee Centre

School

Police

22 Th

aterworks (silk, corn collar manufacture

Elm Barns

Windywold

Boveton Hill

THE SQUARE

5

Broad Close

Paxton Ho.

Borough Terrace

20 Village Hall

CLATTERY

17

26

British Legion Library

Bowls

To Churchill Close

6

19

Rodneys'

Arreton

Bishop's Barn

STAT

21

15

Brooku

School (old)

16

CROWN STREET

The Great Western Arms

Lower Farm

18

7

8

9

Sh

Tally-ho Corner

19 Porch House

Crown Inn

8 Blockley C (silk

18 Lowerbrook Hotel

Bishop's Fish Pond

W N S E

7 Colebrook House (silk)

9 Sn (sil

orks

Park Farm

Prinknash Abbey Pottery
Tel: Painswick 812455
Open: all year, *Pottery* Monday-
Saturday 10am–4.30pm, Sunday 2–5pm,
Pottery Shop daily 10am–6pm.

Sudeley Castle
Nr Winchcombe
Tel: Winchcombe 602308
Whitsun Holiday, Festival of Crafts
with exhibitions and demonstrations.

OTHER PLACES OF INTEREST

Beckford Silk Mill
The Old Vicarage, Beckford
Tel: Evesham 881507
Open: all year, Monday-Friday
9.30am–1pm, 2–6pm. Saturday
2–5.30pm. Closed Bank Holidays

Model Railway
Bourton-on-the-Water
Tel: Bourton-on-the-Water 20686
Open: April to September, daily
11am–5.30pm; October to March,
Saturday and Sunday 11am–5pm, but
daily in school holidays.

Model Village
High Street, Bourton-on-the-Water
Tel: Bourton-on-the-Water 20467
Open: all year, summer daily 9am–7pm
or dusk.

The Perfumery
Bourton-on-the-Water
Tel: Bourton-on-the-Water 20698
Open: all year: summer, daily
9am–dusk; winter, daily 9am–5pm.

OTHER BUILDINGS AND ITEMS OF
INTEREST

Banbury Stone
Bredon Hill

Curfew Tower
Moreton-in-Marsh

Devil's Chimney
Leckhampton Hill

Four-Shire Stone
On the A44 two miles east of Moreton-
in-Marsh

Frampton-on-Severn
Largest village green in England

King and Queen Stones
Bredon Hill

Nailsworth Ladder
An exceptionally steep road out of the
town

Tyndale Monument
North Nibley

Painswick
Fine collection of yew trees in the church
and England's finest collection of table-
top tombs, many finely sculptured.
Tomb Trail leaflets available

Sapperton Tunnel
Portals at Sapperton and Coates. Tunnel,
more than 2 miles long, on Thames and
Severn Canal.

Seven Springs
Source of the River Churn (and/or
Thames).

Severn Bore
Tidal race along the river, best seen at
Stonebench.

Somerset Monument
Hawkesbury Upton

Thameshead
Nr Coates
Source of the River Thames

Tortworth Chestnut
Tortworth Church

Town Stocks
Market Square, Stow-on-the-Wold

Town Stocks
Nr Painswick Church

Town Stocks
Town Hall, Winchcombe

Three-Shire Stone
On Foss Way north of Batheaston, nr Bath

BRASS RUBBINGS

===

Brass Rubbing Centre.
Corn Hall, Cirencester
Tel: Cirencester 4180
Open: all year, daily 10am–6pm.

Brass Rubbing Centre
The Cathedral, Gloucester
Open: July and August, Monday–Saturday and 10am–5pm, Sunday 2–5pm

In addition some churches will allow rubbings to be made (notably Northleach, Tormarton, and Wotton-under-Edge) but permission *must* be obtained before commencing work

---

TOURIST INFORMATION CENTRES

===

The majority of the Cotswolds falls within the area of the Heart of England Tourist Board, whose main office is at:
The Heart of England Tourist Board
PO Box 15
Worcester WR1 2JT

Other offices are at:

8 Abbey Churchyard
Bath
Tel: Bath (0225) 62831
Open: all year, Monday-Saturday
10am–5.30pm.

Municipal Offices
The Promenade, Cheltenham
Tel: Cheltenham (0242) 522878
Open: all year, Monday-Friday
9.30am–6.30pm, Saturday 9.30am–5pm,
Sunday 10am–1pm.

The Corn Hall
Market Place, Cirencester
Tel: Cirencester (0285) 4180
Open: October to May, Monday-Friday
10am–1pm and 2–4pm; June to
September, Monday-Friday 10am–5pm,
Saturday 10am–4pm.

St Michael's Tower
The Cross, Gloucester
Tel: Gloucester (0452) 421188
Open: all year, Monday-Thursday
10am–5pm, Friday 10am–6pm,
Saturday 10am–3.30pm.

Council Offices
High Street, Moreton-in-Marsh
Tel: Moreton-in-Marsh (0608) 50881
Open: all year, Monday-Friday
9am–1pm, 2–5pm.

Council Offices
High Street, Stroud
Tel: Stroud (04536) 4252
Open: all year, Monday-Friday
8.45am–12.45pm, 1.30–5pm.

The Crescent
Tewkesbury
Tel: Tewkesbury (0684) 295027
Open: June to September, daily
10am–4pm; May to October, Monday-
Friday 10am–4pm.

WALKING

===

In addition to the walks described in the book the visitor might like to join a walk organised by the Warden Service of the Cotswold AONB, and led by one their number. Details of the walks programme for each of the four areas of the Cotswold covered by the service (north, central, south and Avon valley) can be obtained from local libraries, or by sending a sae to:

Gloucester County Council
Planning Department
Shire Hall, Gloucester
Tel: Gloucester 21444

Within the area the towns of Gloucester, Cheltenham and Burford offer guided walks around the main sites of interest, and further towns are expected to follow their lead. The Tourist Information Offices will supply details of the year's programmes.

There are two long-distance footpaths that have sections within the AONB. The Cotswold Way is entirely within the area. It is 100 miles long and follows the escarpment closely from Chipping Campden to Bath. The Oxfordshire Way is a 60 mile path linking Bourton-on-the-Water with the Chilterns.

LOCAL EVENTS

Bisley
May. On Ascension Day the Village Well is blessed to appease the water spirits

Bourton-on-the-Water
August. On Bank Holiday Monday a six-a-side football match is played. The game is played to strict FA rules, the only difference from a normal match being that it is played in the River Windrush

Cooper's Hill
May. On Spring Bank Holiday Monday the traditional cheese rolling takes place down the 200yd slope.

Dover's Hill
June. A modern version of Robert Dover's 'Olympick' Games takes place on the hill, at the time of the Scuttlebrook Wake in Chipping Campden

Gloucester
April. On St George's Day the Mummers perform their ancient plays around the city

Painswick
September. On the Sunday nearest 19 September the Church is clipped, or encircled, by the parishoners, the children carrying flowers

Stow-on-the-Wold
May and October. The ancient sheep fairs now concentrate on the sale of horses.

Stroud
July. A truly international event. As part of the traditional Stroud Show there are brick and rolling pin throwing competitions between the Strouds of England, USA and Australia.

Tetbury
May. On Spring Bank Holiday Monday relay teams carry a 50lb woolsack up and down the steepest streets. A reminder of the Cotswolds' woollen past!

In addition there are the famous Cheltenham Music and Literature Festivals, and the Bath Arts Festival. Many of the Cotswolds' villages hold summer fairs which the visitor may also visit.

SPORTS

Sports Centres

Bath, Sports and Leisure Centre, North Parade Road
Tel: Bath 62563
Bristol, There are several centres within the city
Cheltenham, Bourneside Warden Hill Road
Tel: Cheltenham 39123
Cirencester, Tetbury Road.
Tel: Cirencester 4057

135

Gloucester, Station Road.
Tel: Gloucester 36498
Stroud, Stratford Park.
Tel: Stroud 6771
Tewkesbury, Tewkesbury School.
Tel: Tewkesbury 293953

Swimming Pools
Bath, Beau Street,
Tel: Bath 25594
Bath Street,
Tel: Bath 25321
Bristol, many within the city.
Cheltenham, Sandford Park,
Tel: Cheltenham 24430
Tommy Taylor's Lane,
Tel: Cheltenham 28764
Cirencester outdoor at Cecily Hill
Tel: Cirencester 3947
Indoor at Tetbury Road
Tel: Cirencester 4057
Gloucester The Leisure Centre
Tel: Gloucester 36498
Stroud indoor and outdoor at the
Leisure Centre, Stratford Park.
Tel: Stroud 6771
Tewkesbury Oldbury Road.
Tel: Tewkesbury 293740

Golf
Bath Golf Club, Sham Castle
Tel: Bath 25182 Broadway Golf Course,
Willersley Hill
Tel: Broadway 3561
Burford Golf Club, Burford
Tel: Burford 2149
Chipping Sodbury Golf Club, Horton
Road
Tel: Chipping Sodbury 319024
Cirencester Golf Course, Cheleham
Road, Bagendon
Tel: Cirencester 3939
Cleeve Hill Golf Course, Cleeve Hill
Tel: Bishop's Cleeve 2025
Cotswold Edge Golf Club, Wotton-
under-Edge
Tel: Dursley 844167
Cotswold Hills Golf Course, Ullenwood
Tel: Cheltenham 522421
Gloucester Golf Club, Matson Lane
Tel: Gloucester 25653

Lansdown Golf Club, Lansdown
Tel: Bath 25007
Lilley Brook Golf Course, Charlton
Kings
Tel: Cheltenham 26785
Minchinhampton Old Course,
Minchinhampton
Tel: Nailsworth 2642
Minchinhampton New Course,
Minchinhampton
Tel: Nailsworth 3866
Painswick Golf Course, Painswick
Tel: Painswick 2180
Stinchcombe Golf Course, Stinchcombe
Hill
Tel: Dursley 2015
Tewkesbury Park Golf and Country
Club
Lincoln Green Lane
Tel: Tewkesbury 295405

Fishing
The rivers leading down to the Thames
valley offer very good trout fishing, as
do the reservoirs to the west of Bath.
Elsewhere in the area there is good
coarse fishing. All fishing is controlled
by private owners or clubs, but permits
can be arranged at some local hotels or
by contacting club secretaries direct.
Course and Game fishing is also
available at the Cotswold Water Park

Riding
The Cotswolds are not a centre for pony
trekking as there is only a limited
amount of common land. There are,
however, a number of excellent riding
schools within the area.

Boating
Canal boats may be hired from points
along the northern Avon, at Tewkesbury
and Bredon for example, to explore the
river and the canal system around it.
Boats may also be hired for outings on
the Avon at Bath and other points along
its length, and at Lechlade and nearby
points for the River Thames.

136

Water Sports
The Cotswold Water Park covering 14,000 acres of open water on two sites around Fairford and Ashton Keynes/South Cerney (south of Cirencester) has a wide variety of water-based clubs. The visitor should arrange permission to use the facilities before his trip. There are regular spectator sports. Park activities include sailing, rowing, hydro-plane racing, water skiing and fishing.
Contact the Tourist Office, Cirencester

Cycling
The Cotswolds are an excellent centre for cycling and those who do not wish to bring their own cycles may hire them at many of the bigger towns. A full list of hire facilities for each season is available from the Tourist Information Centres.

Skiing
At Robinswood Hill, near Gloucester, is England's longest dry ski run. Courses are available at all levels and use of the run may be possible for visitors.
Tel: Gloucester 414300

Gliding
Gliding courses are available from the Bristol and Gloucestershire Gliding Club at Frocester Hill, Nympsfield, nr Stonehouse
Tel: Uley 343

Spectator Sports
Gloucester County Cricket Club play matches at Bristol, Cheltenham and Gloucester, with very occasional matches at Moreton-in-the-Marsh
Both Gloucester, Cheltenham and Bath have excellent Rugby teams.
There is horse racing at Cheltenham — the Gold Cup meeting is in March, and at the Lansdown Race Course, Bath. There are also numerous point-to-point meetings in the area, most notably at Stow and Broadway in April and Woodford, near Dursley, in May. Lovers of equestrian events will need little introduction to the Badminton

Three-Day Event in April, and the polo matches at Cirencester Park on Sundays throughout the Summer.
At Castle Combe the racing circuit is used about four times annually for car racing while the Prescott hill-climbs, near Cheltenham, are held about three times each year. The foremost Prescott meet is the vintage event in August. Motor cycle scramble meets are held at a variety of places throughout the year.

NATURE RESERVES

There are many nature reserves within the Cotswolds area, some with associated nature trails. Other sites may be visited by permit. Full details are available from:

Gloucestershire Trust for Nature Conservation
Church House
Standish, nr Stonehouse
Gloucestershire
Tel: Stonehouse 2761

Avon Wildlife Trust 209 Redland Road
Bristol
Tel: Bristol 743396

Wiltshire Trust for Nature Conservation
Wyndhams
St Josephs Place
Devizes
Tel: Devizes 5669

COTSWOLD WARDEN SERVICE

The Cotswold AONB has a Warden Service consisting of both full and part-time wardens. They offer a programme of guided walks and farms open days, and are also on hand at some places of interest mentioned above to offer help and information. They also assist in the up-keep of footpaths. Details of all warden services are available from:

THE VISITOR'S GUIDE SERIES